TIDY HACKS

Handy Hints to Make Life Easier

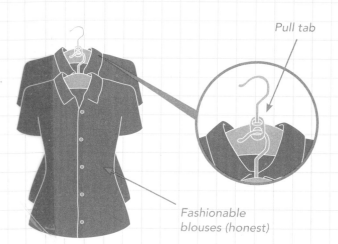

Pull tab

*Fashionable
blouses (honest)*

Dan Marshall

HARPER
DESIGN

An Imprint of HarperCollins*Publishers*

DISCLAIMER

Neither the author nor the publisher can be held responsible for any loss or claim arising out of the use, or misuse, of the suggestions made herein.

TIDY HACKS

Copyright © Summersdale Publishers Ltd, 2016

Research and illustrations by Rob Melhuish

Published in 2016 by
Harper Design
An Imprint of HarperCollins*Publishers*
195 Broadway
New York, NY 10007
Tel: (212) 207-7000
Fax: (855) 746-6023
harperdesign@harpercollins.com
www.hc.com

Distributed throughout North America by
HarperCollins*Publishers*
195 Broadway
New York, NY 10007

ISBN 978-0-06-265421-2

Library of Congress Control Number: 2016955777

Printed in the United States of America

First Printing, 2016

TIDY
HACKS

CONTENTS

Introduction 7

Kitchen Hacks 8

Bathroom Hacks 40

Bedroom Hacks 56

Desk Hacks 85

Laundry Hacks 93

General Household Hacks 106

Garden Hacks 125

Kids' Hacks 150

Multiple-Use Hacks 158

Arts-and-Crafts Hacks 170

DIY Hacks 176

Final Word 187

Index 188

INTRODUCTION

Welcome to *Tidy Hacks*, the book for anyone who longs to be free from those horribly time-consuming everyday household chores. Whether you're a domestic demon with little time on your hands or totally disinclined with a duster or DIY, dozens of everyday tidying dilemmas are solved with this handy guide to tackling domestic annoyances, cheaply and swiftly, so you can get on with something more fun and fulfilling instead.*

So if you have taken to piling your clothes up on the floor rather than tackling your overflowing cupboards and drawers, or your carpets have changed color due to the amount of dog hair woven into them, or perhaps you've lost one too many socks in the washing machine, then this handy guide has a hack for you, covering everything from ingenious space-saving storage solutions, clever cleaning hacks, DIY, and much, much more.

*Snacks and beer round the pool, anyone?

KITCHEN HACKS

The heart of the house can often become a scene of chaos and destruction, but that's hardly surprising when you think of the daily assault it endures. Remain calm and get order back in no time with these time-saving and organizational hacks, from tidying shortcuts using desk organizers to clever ways to declutter.

EASY-EMPTY GARBAGE CAN

At home it's my job to empty the garbage, and boy do I hate it! When you have stuffed as much in there as humanly possible, trying to get the bag out can be tricky. This is due to the vacuum that is created when trying to yank out the garbage bag. To rectify this little problem get your power drill out.

Drill a couple of holes in the bottom of the garbage can to stop the vacuum from ever forming. The bag will now lift out with ease.

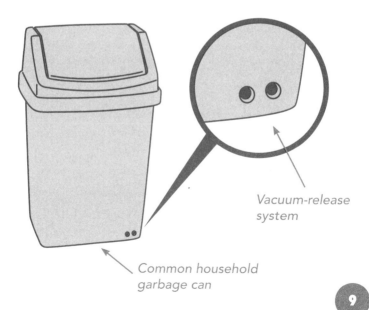

*Vacuum-release
system*

*Common household
garbage can*

JAMMY STORAGE

Are you the kind of person who owns lots of tiny pointless things? Me too! I have found a new *tidy* way to store them. You'll be feeling pretty jammy once you know how....

If you have recently been to a posh hotel, I bet you anything that you've bagged quite a few of those little jam jars that make your stay all the more enjoyable; along with the batteries in the TV remote and perhaps as many toiletries as you could cram into your bag....However, if you are wondering what on earth to do with these jars, other than fill them with small amounts of jam, then here is a handy alternative.

Drill a small hole in the center of each jam jar lid, then nail or screw them to the underside of shelving or cabinets, near to an area where tiny things lurk; fill the jars up and screw them back onto the lids.

Teeny-tiny jam jars

Even tinier knickknacks

PIN-UP FREEZER BAG BOXES

Slightly different from the usual pin-up pose, these freezer bag boxes could be misplaced, damaged, or even permanently lost if it wasn't for their all-new starring role in the pantry.

When it's time to make a packed lunch, freezer bags are known to disappear. So to keep them in position, tack the box lid to a wall or the inside of a cupboard door, anywhere that will be useful to grab the sandwich bags, and go.

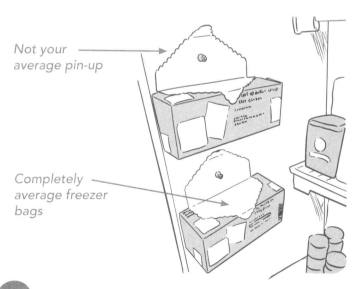

Not your average pin-up

Completely average freezer bags

SUPER STORAGE HANGER

Clearing out the shoe closet? If you don't happen to be doing that, then just throw away your shoes and get started! These over-the-door shoe racks are really handy for storing almost anything: cleaning equipment, crafty bits and bobs, bathroom clutter, and children's toys. Plus, it's easy too, just put your hanger on the inside of a full-length closet door (the pantry door is ideal) and dump your clutter into the compartments; you'll look like a true tidying professional, *and* the best news is, you get to close the door so you won't ever have to look at it again!

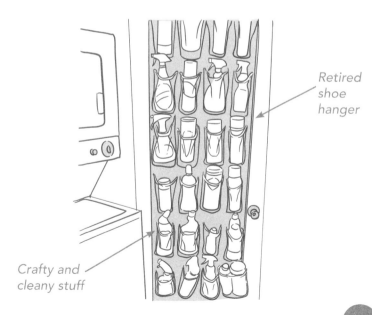

Retired shoe hanger

Crafty and cleany stuff

DESK-TO-FRIDGE ORGANIZER

Ever found yourself fumbling around the fridge, over empty jars of mayonnaise, tubs of butter you forgot you had, and jars of millennial chutney? Your mission was to find the pesto you were sure you had, but it turns out it's nowhere to be seen; it's completely vanished, and it's Pasta Wednesday! D'oh!

Here is a simple solution: use desk organizers in the fridge and freezer to arrange your food. You will be able to fit more in...plus, you will know exactly what you have, and how much, if similar foods are all kept in the same place. What a genius idea, even if I do say so myself.

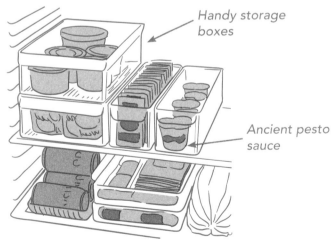

Handy storage boxes

Ancient pesto sauce

BASKET SPACE

Simple and yet oh-so effective, hanging baskets onto the back of cupboard doors creates more space for your things. Plastic or woven doesn't matter, as long as they have open spaces big enough to hang from a hook. It is also a brilliant way to organize bits and bobs without having to have them on display.

All you will need are some hooks (adhesive or screw-in, at least two for each basket), a few baskets, and the back of a cupboard door. Attach two hooks onto the back of the door (around the length of your basket) and attach the basket to it.

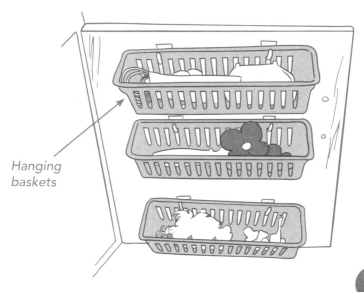

Hanging baskets

BOOKENDS FOR BEER BOTTLES

In the summertime, my Saturday after-noons feel more like a beer festival than anything else. Barbecues, patio doors open all day; come rain or shine I will be holding a cool bottle and sporting a pair of palm tree shorts and flip-flops.

Of course, I keep my bottles efficiently stacked in the fridge on their sides, all the better to get more in—until disaster strikes. The bottles of beer roll off one another, straight onto the steaks; now they are fizzy, or worse, broken.

To stop the madness and preserve the beers simply use a binder clip, like a sort of bottle bookend. Slide the clip onto the shelf, with the top prong lying along the shelf. The clip part will act as a barrier and stop the stacked bottles from moving. You are now free to enjoy summer with total peace of mind...in the beer department anyway.

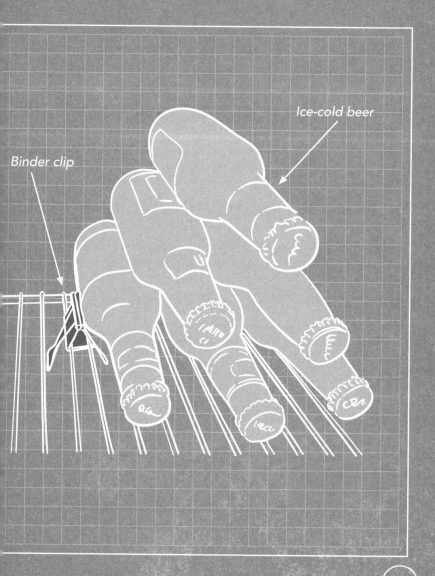

Binder clip

Ice-cold beer

COOKIE JAR

We all seem to acquire junk. No matter how hard we try to get rid of it, it just keeps turning up and some of it could be even useful.

Things like cables, pens, Post-It notes, etc. can be hidden away in a clever hiding place–the cookie jar. It might confuse your guests when they search your kitchen for snacks, but the cookie jar is a great place to hide all your ugly but useful stuff.

A really useful container masquerading as an amusingly shaped cookie jar

MONEY BOX

Do you sometimes worry that your trousers are going to fall down under the weight of the loose coins in your pockets? Then here's the perfect hack for you. Use takeout containers to store your spare change. Cut a slot in each lid and use each container for a different coin denomination. It is a nifty way to save your pennies; plus, you can now walk around, light as a feather.

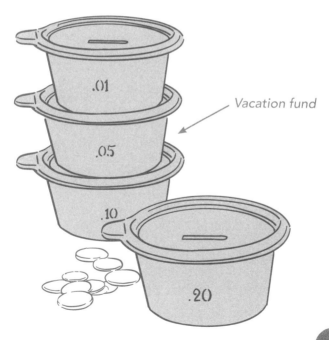

Vacation fund

CUPCAKE LINERS JAM JARS

If, like me, you love baking cupcakes but when searching for paper liners they're all crushed at the back of the drawer, then let me suggest the perfect hack. Instead of shoving these lovely things in a drawer or cupboard, stack them in a jam jar, screw on the lid, and put them away until the next time you need them. How easy is that?

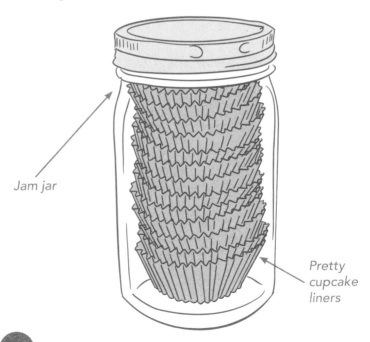

Jam jar

Pretty cupcake liners

GARBAGE BAG ROLLERS

Every one of us knows how great toilet-paper-roll holders are, so why isn't there one for household garbage bags too? I have acknowledged this issue and created a simple hack for those of you who want to do garbage bags in style.

All you need are some long hooks (just long enough to let the garbage bags spin freely) and a dowel rod or something similar. Push the dowel through the garbage bag liner roll and then onto the hook. You might be lucky enough to have some long hooks or dowels lying around (or stashed in a cookie jar, see page 18), but if you are not, they are readily available at DIY shops up and down the land for very little cost.

So there you have it, all that remains is to put the roller inside your cupboards for better bag duty.

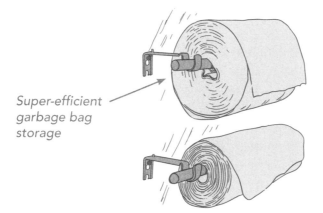

Super-efficient garbage bag storage

OVER-THE-SINK CHOPPING BOARD

Do your work surfaces fill up quickly when you're cooking and you find yourself chopping veggies on the top of your washing machine? I did, until I made myself an over-the-sink hardwood chopping board!

STEP ONE: Choosing the right type of hardwood is an essential stage in what will be the best for your kitchen....I know, I sound like an ancient wizard explaining the importance of wand wood. Anyway, once it is chosen you can get on with the rest.

STEP TWO: Measure the width and breadth of the sink. Make sure your board is slightly longer than the long edges of your sink so you can slot the board over it comfortably. However, keep it a little narrower than the breadth, otherwise the overhang won't fit.

STEP THREE: On the underside of the board, about a half inch from the short edge, mark a line going all the way across. This is where you are going to make your ledge so the board sits almost flat with the sink/surface. Use a table saw to cut down about a quarter inch along the line into the board (make sure you don't go all the way through!), then flip the board breadthways and also cut about a quarter inch from the edge, remove the excess wood and you have yourself a nifty ledge. Repeat on the opposite end. Sand it and treat it with beeswax, mineral oil, or coconut oil.

STEP FOUR: You don't want the board to slip around too much (lost fingers are never a good look). So drill a couple of holes, find a few rubber stoppers of the right size, and insert them into the holes.

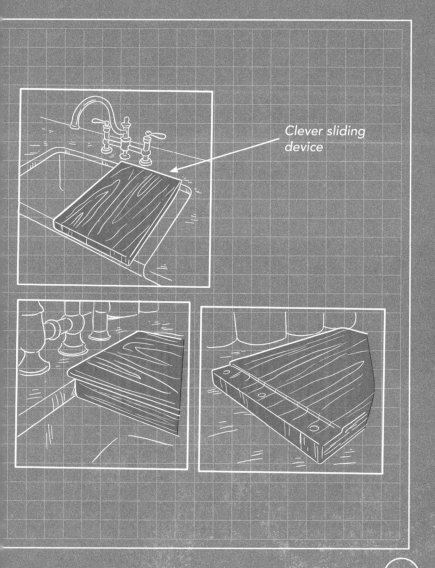

Clever sliding device

23

VELCRO PLUGS

Most vacuum cleaners have got it right: push a button and the cord is sucked back into the machine. But clearly the iron, slow cooker, portable heater, and hair dryer manufacturers didn't get the memo.

Well, I've got a solution up my sleeve and that is Velcro. Stick one side of the Velcro onto the plug, and the other onto the appliance. Then when you wind the cord around the heater or iron, you can stick the plug in place and store your item away tidily. No more loose cords.

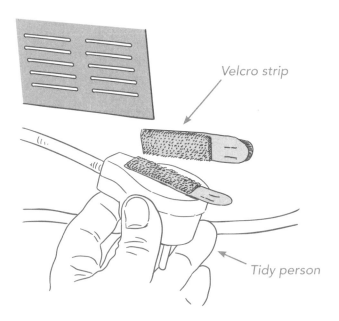

Velcro strip

Tidy person

PLASTIC BAG DISPENSER

Are your plastic bags becoming a bit unruly? Are they stuffed into nooks and crannies all over the kitchen? Time to take back control! All you need is an empty plastic wet wipe dispenser.

To put the bags correctly into the plastic tube so that when a bag is taken from the dispenser it comes out handle up, with another waiting ready in its place, here's what to do. Lay one bag down flat so there is no air left inside. Fold in half lengthways, handle to handle. Lay down another bag over the first bag and fold likewise, so its handle overlaps the bottom of the first bag. Do this for ten more bags. After the last bag, fold the first handle outward so it sticks up and roll them up as tightly as you can. Insert into the dispenser and just like that you have a carrier bag dispenser.

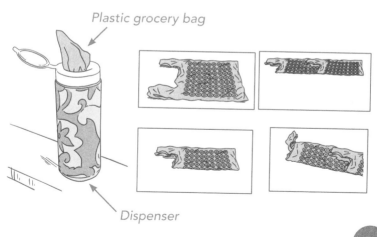

Plastic grocery bag

Dispenser

THE LAZY MICROWAVE-CLEANING TRICK

If the inside of your microwave looks and smells like a week-old diaper then this next hack will be a godsend.

Halve a lemon and put it into a glass dish or jug, along with some water. Microwave it until the water starts to boil, then turn off the microwave and leave the door closed for a minute or two while the lemony steam works its magic. You should find that last night's Bolognese can be wiped off effortlessly—and that unholy smell has disappeared. Stick a copy of this tip to the office microwave (there's always one person who eats exploding soup for lunch). A clean kitchen is a happy one!

Grime-blasting steam

Lemon

Jug

GRAPEFRUIT OVEN CLEANER

You might hate the sour taste of a grapefruit, but I'm willing to bet you'll love how well it cleans your oven!

Get down to the supermarket and buy yourself a large grapefruit (you can make believe that you're a health freak who simply adores eating unpalatable foods). Cut the grapefruit into two halves, then cover the sticky fruit end in salt, either rock salt or table salt will do, and give your oven a good old scrub. It will cut through grime and grease in no time, leaving the oven with an all-important fresh smell too!

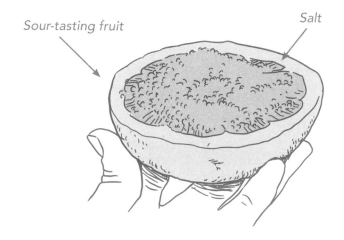

Sour-tasting fruit

Salt

TOMATO POLISH

Polishing pans with ketchup? What planet are we on, you say? Well prepare to be truly surprised–this staple really does have the power to buff up your pots and pans.

Spread a thin layer of sauce onto the offending piece of cookware and rub it in. Resisting the urge to lick, leave it to work for thirty minutes. Something called acetic acid will react with the oxides that have caused your pans to discolor. When you wipe it off you will reveal the sparkling surface of the pan you once knew! Now, who wants fries?

Dull pan

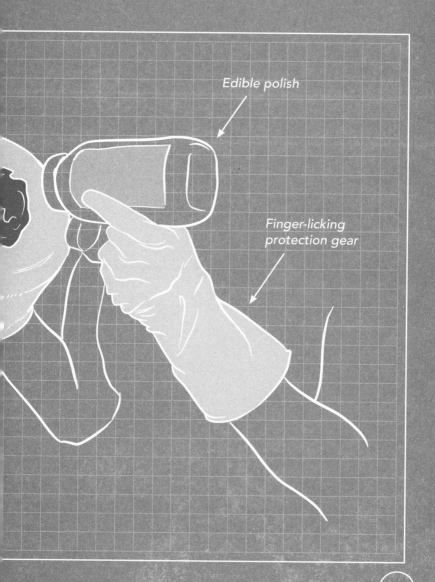

Edible polish

Finger-licking
protection gear

SAUCEPAN LID ORGANIZER

I can never find the right lid to fit the pan I'm using, it's like they go out of their way to hide or something. If you share this annoying experience, here's an elegant solution.

Grab some of those sticky hooks (the plastic kind you can hang pictures with) and make a selection of mini saucepan racks on the inside of your cupboard door. Make sure you space them correctly, so the lids rest on the hooks. And remember not to slam the door!

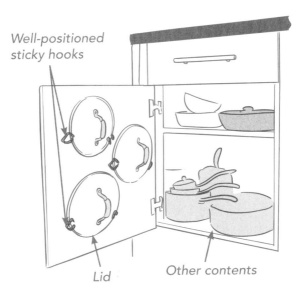

Well-positioned sticky hooks

Lid

Other contents

DRAIN DECLOGGER

If an eggy smell starts to penetrate the kitchen then you have been warned…your drains are clogged, probably with the moldy curry sauce you threw down there.

Free your drains of dirt and germs that make a stink and clog your pipes! Fill the sink up to just above halfway with warm water and add one cup of vinegar and half a cup of baking soda. Mix together and then pull the plug! This will blast away any stale food you might have lurking down there and any smells that come with it.

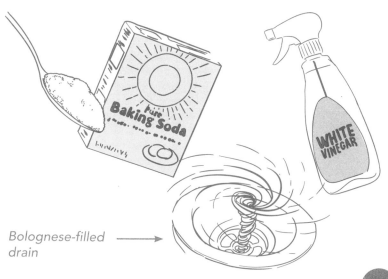

Bolognese-filled drain

CLEANER COFFEE

Experiencing eye-wateringly sour coffee from your coffee machine? (No, it isn't supposed to taste like that.) Here's a simple hack to clean your coffee machine.

Fill the water tank with white vinegar, place a receptacle under the nozzle, then let your coffee machine run through as normal (without the coffee, obviously!). You should see brownish liquid being dispensed, which is all the dirt and old coffee being washed out. Keep running it until the vinegar coming out is clear.

To remove the vinegar residue, empty and wash out the water container and fill it again, this time with water. Run through until the container is near empty. Fill again and run through once more for luck; a simple recipe for better coffee.

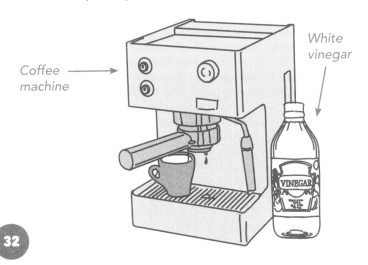

Coffee machine

White vinegar

VINEGAR

SQUEAKY-CLEAN SPONGES

Prolong the life of your sponges by disinfecting them. Sounds stupid, doesn't it? But, if you think about it, you can't really clean with something that's already dirty—and sponges, being porous, are prone to carrying bacteria.

To make sure you're not spreading more germs than you're eliminating, simply hold your sponge under the tap until it's full of water. Then pop it in the microwave on full power for two minutes. Leave it in there for a while, so your hands don't boil when you pick it up, and when it's cool you have a sanitized sponge (unless your microwave is all gross—but we already gave you a hack for that!).

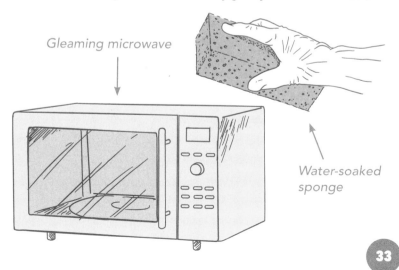

Gleaming microwave

Water-soaked sponge

BURNT-PAN CLEANER

It happens to everyone: you're in the middle of cooking when the phone rings and you answer it, thinking it's your partner with news of a lottery win. Five minutes later, when you return to your pan, the contents look like a scene from a disaster movie. (And to cap it all, it was someone selling life insurance and you're still not a millionaire... great!) Fortunately, you can bring your blackened pan back to life without the use of eye-watering chemicals.

Fill the pan with an inch of water and add 250 ml (one cup) of white vinegar. Heat until the solution comes to a boil. After three or four minutes, turn off the heat and add 30–45 ml (two to three tablespoons) of baking soda. Give it a stir, then stand back and let the baking soda work its fizzy magic. After a few minutes, empty the pan and scrub any burnt bits that are left— they should come away fairly easily, leaving you with a sparkling pan. I've scorched more pans than I care to think about. This hack saves my bacon every time!

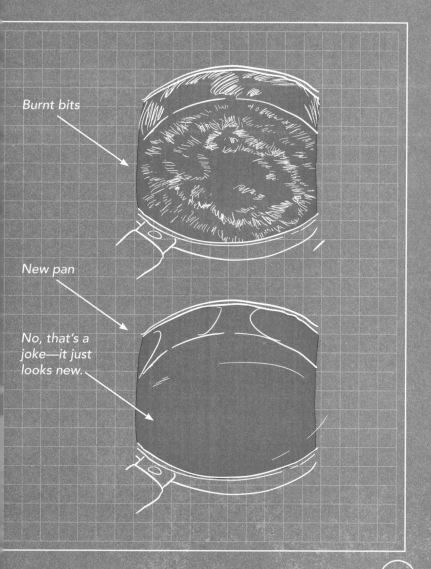

Burnt bits

New pan

No, that's a joke—it just looks new.

KNIFE AND FORK RUST REMOVER

Personally, I just ask my butler, Ralph, to polish the silverware at least once a week. But if you don't have a butler, there's a neat way to get rid of those horrid rust spots that often appear after you've put your knives through a dishwasher. Grab some lemon juice from the fridge (or ask Ralph to squeeze some fresh lemons) and pour the juice into a tall glass. Soak your rusted cutlery in the lemon juice for a few minutes. The acid in the lemon will help to loosen up the rust, making it easier to scrub off. Works like a charm! (Just make sure you dry the cutlery thoroughly afterwards, otherwise you're asking for trouble.)

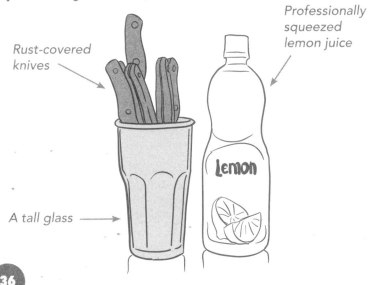

Professionally squeezed lemon juice

Rust-covered knives

Lemon

A tall glass

BANISH KITCHEN ODORS

You're a maestro in the kitchen and your fish-head curry was a big hit! But the next morning your house smells like a garbage can. You could open every single window in the house and freeze to death, or you could use this hack.

Preheat your oven to its lowest setting and pour two caps of vanilla extract into an ovenproof dish. Place the dish in the oven and sniff appreciatively as the scent of baking cookies wafts throughout the house. Sure, baking real cookies would have the same effect, but that takes time and effort–time and effort you expended when making your fish-head curry!

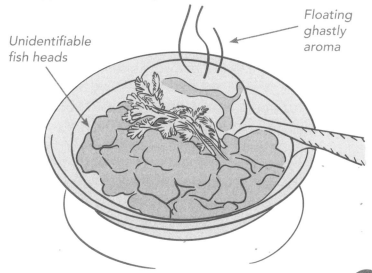

Floating ghastly aroma

Unidentifiable fish heads

QUICK-AS-A-FLASH BLENDER CLEANER

Facepalm alert: I like a broccoli-and-banana smoothie as much as the next person, but I'm not so keen on cleaning the blender afterwards. I use a simple trick to make cleaning a cinch.

It's so obvious you'll kick yourself for not thinking of it. Just fill the blender with warm water. Add a squirt of dishwashing liquid, blend for a few seconds, then rinse the jug with warm water and dry. A perfectly clean blender with no goo or gunk left to scrub out. Anyone else feel a bit stupid?

Goo-less blender

Dishwashing liquid

TENSION ROD HANGER

Here's a genius space-saver for storing your cleaning products! Hang cleaning products from a tension rod in your under-sink cupboard—dangling your cleaning products from a height might sound like a strange idea, but it may just actually create some more space in the cupboard, leaving your most-used spray bottles hanging on the rod and ready to use.

Wedge a length of thick dowel rod or a metal or plastic tube across the top of your cupboard. Make sure it's in there tightly and then you can get hanging. You can color coordinate them, hang them worst to most effective, in exact order of cleaning, room to room, or you can just sit and admire your great handiwork, either way a tension rod will give your cleaning regime a boost.

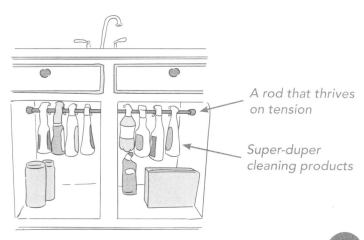

A rod that thrives on tension

Super-duper cleaning products

BATHROOM HACKS

The place in the house where we go to wash simply has to be clean—end of story. There's nothing worse than grimy grout between the tiles, a toxic toilet or a pile of soggy towels piled up on the floor. As our bathrooms are also generally the smallest rooms in our homes, it's important they're spic-and-span and super-organized, so we can concentrate on the task at hand and create our own little oasis of calm.

TOWEL HOOKS

Ever thought of hanging something other than coats on coat hooks? Are you sick and tired of coming into the bathroom and finding your towel slung on the floor to make room for someone else's? It would have to be yours, wouldn't it? If you hadn't already guessed it, the answer is hang your towels on coatracks. You can fit two fluffy towels on one hook instead, they make your bathroom look pretty neat, and you can put up as many as you like...well maybe not too many, but you get the gist. Cool!

Wonder hooks

Towels— no longer on the floor

HOMEMADE CLEANER

Bathroom cleaning products can be expensive, so why fork out when you can use everyday household items to create your own. "What?!" I hear you cry. It's true.

Fill an old spray bottle with two-thirds vinegar and one-third dishwashing liquid and you have just made your own limescale-beating bathroom cleaner. Unfortunately, you will still have to use a considerable amount of elbow grease to scrub the scum from your bathtub....

SUDS

Dishwashing liquid

Spray bottle for easy application

Vinegar

SHOWER STORAGE

Have you got enough toiletries to set up your very own chain of bath and body shops? They've stopped selling men's bath soap in bulk but otherwise I would. I've now stocked up on Brillo pads, great as an exfoliator (only joking!), so I found an ingenious way to store them. If you hang an extra shower curtain rod in your shower you will find that you can use it to hang baskets to store all of your bathroom essentials.

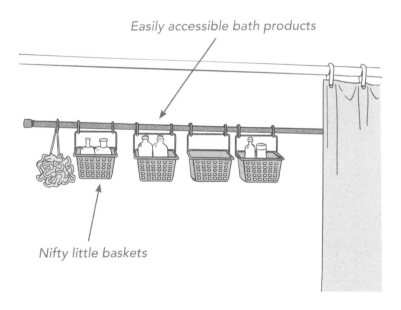

Easily accessible bath products

Nifty little baskets

SPACE-SAVING TOWEL STORAGE

If your bathroom is barely large enough to swing a cat, storage is always going to be a problem.

If so, don't fret. Borrow this tip from experienced backpackers: choose rolling instead of folding. Do this with your bathroom towels and store them on a shelf or in a nice wicker basket. Eureka! A hack that is both functional and decorative. Your bathroom will look like a budget spa too!

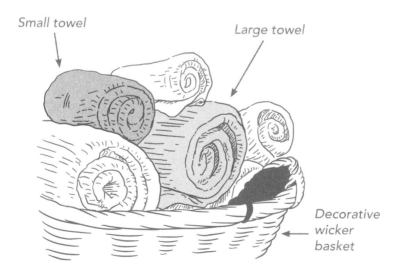

Small towel

Large towel

Decorative wicker basket

007 TOWEL HANGING

A guest once called my bathroom "bijou": I think what this word really means is tiny. So, if you've got a microscopic–I mean, *bijou*–bathroom like me, then this hack will really come in handy.

Fix multiple small towel rods onto the back of the bathroom door. When the door is open your towels and hand towels are nowhere to be seen and when you need them–hopefully you close your door when using the bathroom–they will appear. Very 007.

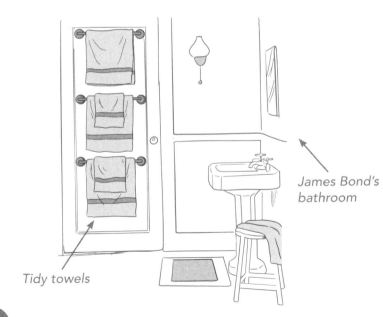

James Bond's bathroom

Tidy towels

FRUIT BASKET BATHROOM

Here's a way to make children's toys look attractive. It is admittedly not easy to make a rubber duck, three submarines and a big purple whale look aesthetically pleasing, but I have found a way.

Get a hanging fruit and vegetable basket, the kind with three or four tiers. Hang it from the shower curtain rail, the ceiling or anywhere else that's out of the way. Scoop up the large collection of brightly colored bath toys and put them in the baskets. *Voilà!* It looks jazzy and keeps things tidy, all at the same time.

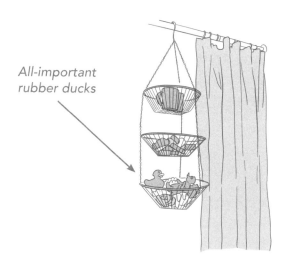

All-important rubber ducks

MAGIC LEMONS

So your bathroom's brand-new, and you vow to yourself that those chrome-finished fittings you insisted on will always look as gleaming as they do now—yeah, right.

My gift to you is lemons. Simply slice a lemon in half and use for your normal bathroom cleaning routine. Rub the half a lemon on your chrome fittings and watch those dull water stains just disappear. Lemons naturally contain citric acid, which breaks down calcium, commonly found in bathrooms—not to mention it kills bacteria. Go lemons!

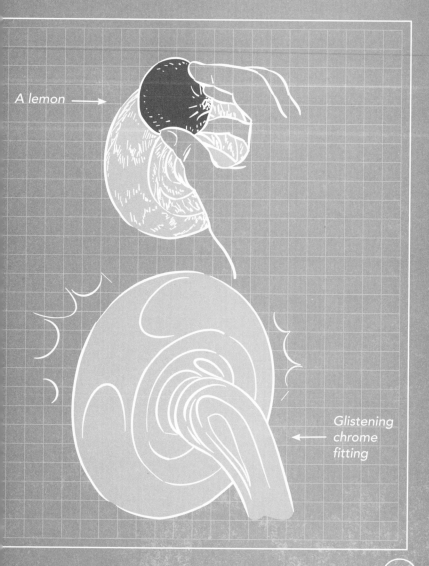

A lemon →

← Glistening chrome fitting

TOOTHPASTE CLIP

Does your partner have irritating bathroom habits? Or are you that annoying person: leaving the toilet seat up, tossing wet towels on the floor, and using the last piece of toilet paper? Many a divorce could have been avoided with better bathroom habits.

I'd say I'm pretty relaxed, though there is one thing that really gets on my nerves and that is a tube of unsqueezed (and unrolled) toothpaste.

If you're a fellow sufferer, get yourself down to the nearest stationery shop and purchase a binder clip. Squeeze the toothpaste, fold over the end of the tube, and clip in place. Squeezed toothpaste = happy marriage.

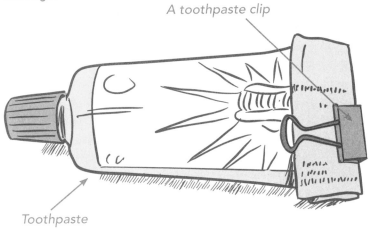

A toothpaste clip

Toothpaste

VINEGAR TOILET CLEANER

Toilet stains are grim. It's almost impossible to remove long-standing stains without the use of weapons-grade plutonium, but luckily there's a nifty solution that is very cheap.

Take one bottle of white distilled vinegar (from supermarkets and DIY stores) and pour a cup or two into the toilet. Swish it around with a toilet brush and leave it to soak for 30 minutes or so. The stain should then come away with a little light scrubbing, leaving your lavatory squeaky clean! Just remember to spritz your bathroom with air freshener so it doesn't smell like you've been eating fish and chips on the toilet.

Grime-ridden toilet

Another bottle of white vinegar

GROUT DE-GRIMER

Grimy grout is the arch nemesis of any bathroom cleaner. Cleaning it seems like it requires some kind of act of god. But you don't need to wait for divine intervention....

Make sure your windows are open, for some much-needed ventilation. Mix together equal parts of baking soda and bleach to form a thick paste (add more baking soda if it's too runny). Smear the paste into the grout and leave to dry overnight. In the morning, use a toothbrush to remove the paste. It may take a few attempts to really blast it away, but eventually you will achieve that holy grail of cleaning victories.

State-of-the-art tiling

bleach

Soda

Bleach

Baking soda

DIY AIR FRESHENER

Your bathroom is not always a haven of sweet-smelling lavender and aromatic bath oils; sometimes it's a little more eau de la stink. So for a bathroom that always smells good have one of these air fresheners on hand. Take a small jar, add baking soda and then ten drops of your favorite essential oil, which can be bought in supermarkets. Cut out a circle of pretty fabric just slightly bigger than the opening of your jar and fasten it with a rubber band. Finally, pierce holes in the material and leave it in a discreet place to do its work of nuking unwelcome smells.

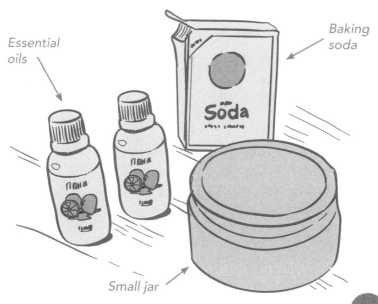

Essential oils

Baking soda

Soda

Small jar

CLEANSING BATHROOM BOMBS

Do you feel like your bath needs a bit of "me time"? No? Well it does—and so does your sink and toilet. Keep them clean with minimal effort by giving them their very own bathroom bombs.

Mix a cup of baking soda and a cup of cream of tartar in a bowl (cream of tartar can be found in health food shops and supermarkets), then add water to bind it together. It should be just sticky enough to form into small bath-bomb-looking shapes. Chuck these into the toilet, bath, and sink when filled with water and let their fizzy magic do the work for you.

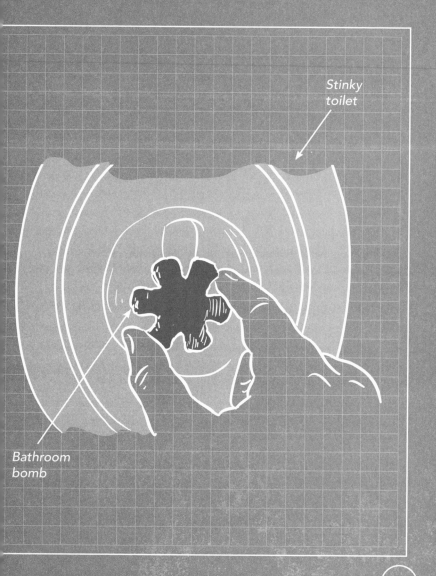

Stinky toilet

Bathroom bomb

BEDROOM HACKS

Most of us could do with a little help in the bedroom department (ha-ha)! Seriously, as much as most of us would love a large, luxurious bedroom, with heaps of hanging space, the truth is most of us are dealing with dreary little spaces with very little storage. Here's how to make your boudoir tip-top.

SMALL-ITEM RETRIEVAL

Where do all those earring backs, watch screws, and contact lenses go when you drop them? I'll tell you where: they're still there, you're just too blind to see them.

When you drop something small and can't find it, grab your vacuum cleaner and a pair of old tights. Slip the tights over the vacuum nozzle and fix in place with a rubber band. Run the vacuum over the area where you think you dropped your item and, with a bit of luck, the item will be sucked onto the tights where you can pick it off with ease. If you find anything of value that isn't yours, just remember this: finders keepers, losers weepers.

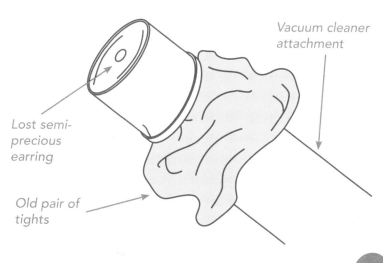

Vacuum cleaner
attachment

Lost semi-
precious
earring

Old pair of
tights

DIY SHOE HANGERS

Shoes have that terrible habit of looking like a bomb's hit them. Somehow even when you place your shoes in the closet neatly at the start of the week, after a few days they have transformed themselves into a mountainous mess. However, I have the perfect solution for making your shoes look tidy all of the time.

First, you will need to hang a rod at the lower part of the closet, leaving enough room between it and the floor for a hanger and shoes to fit. Then find some old, wire coat hangers; these will be fashioned into a very nifty unit for stashing shoes. Locate the center point on the bottom of the hanger and cut with wire cutters. You are left with two separate lengths that you can bend into shape. Bend one half to the left and the other to the right, forming two opposing hook shapes. The ends will be sharp, so twist the ends over to make a hoop or spiral and you have yourself a shoe hanger. Create a hanger for each pair of shoes and hang them up. Happy shoe keeping.

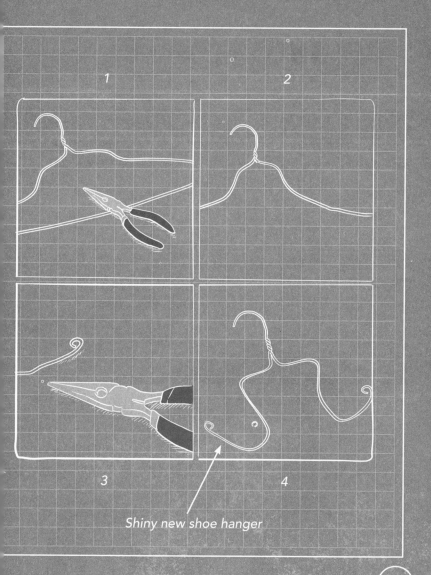

Shiny new shoe hanger

HAIR TIE ORGANIZER

Hair ties can be found covering just about every surface in the bedroom. Hundreds of the things come in the pack and within a few hours, without a doubt, they become strewn across the bedroom, some never to be seen again.

So when enough's enough, get down to your local outdoors shop and purchase (cheaply, of course) what is called a carabiner. These are like big metal clasps usually used for mountain climbing rope. Gather up all the stray hair ties and click the carabiner closed; now they're all in one place and easy to access.

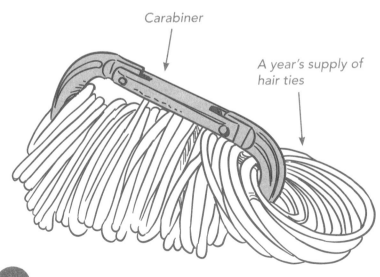

Carabiner

A year's supply of hair ties

ICE CUBE TRAY FOR JEWELRY

No, I don't mean freeze your jewelry, but I do mean put your jewelry in an ice cube tray. (Plastic pillboxes work too.) Rings, earrings, gold chains, and giant cubic zirconia studs will all fit into the compartments.

It will stop your small bits and pieces from getting tangled or lost, and now your favorite necklaces won't get tangled up into one big one.

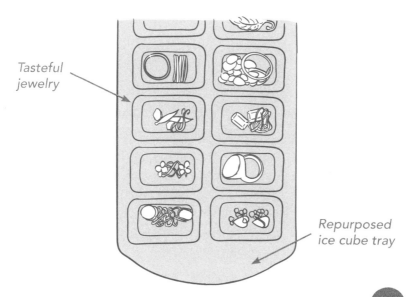

Tasteful jewelry

Repurposed ice cube tray

TEACUP JEWELRY

For a larger man chain, you may need a bigger compartment.

I'm talking about teacups—and the more flowery the better. (Although I am sure you could use one depicting scenes with heavy machinery if you felt you had to.) Using teacups is a good solution for other bits of jewelry, like dangly bracelets and hoop earrings; you can even use the saucer underneath for long necklaces or earrings. They look good on the dressing table and tidy up the jewelry collection.

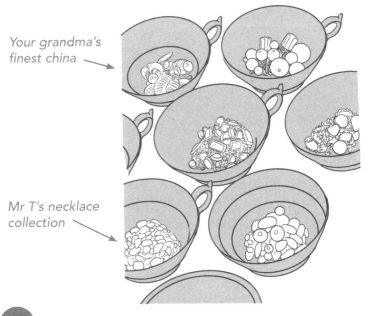

Your grandma's
finest china

Mr T's necklace
collection

EARRING GRATER

It sounds bizarre but this is one of the simplest and best ways to keep your earrings tidy. Begin by sanding down the sharp grating edges of your cheese grater and then paint it with a color of your choosing. This will make it look less like a kitchen utensil and more like a bedroom jewelry accessory stand. Hot-glue four hooks onto the bottom to make feet, and once dry you can hang your earring collection into the holes.

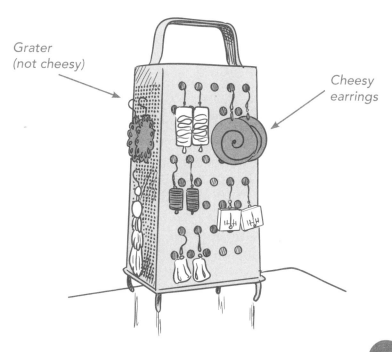

Grater
(not cheesy)

Cheesy
earrings

JEWELRY FIZZ

If you are feeling slightly more adventurous you could make your own jewelry stand. Diamantés aren't cheap and losing one would be heartbreaking to say the least. So here's how to make one.

You will need:
4 plastic bottle ends (two 2-liter plastic bottles, one 1-liter bottle and one 20-ounce bottle)
1 threaded metal rod
8 bolts
8 washers
Electric drill

Start by drilling holes through the center of each bottle end, and then thread one 1-liter end onto the metal rod to form the base. Slide on a washer and screw on a bolt to each side. Do the same with the other 1-liter bottle end but this time turn it the opposite way to the base so that it forms a container. Repeat the same steps with the other two bottle ends. Stand it up and fill with priceless jewelry.

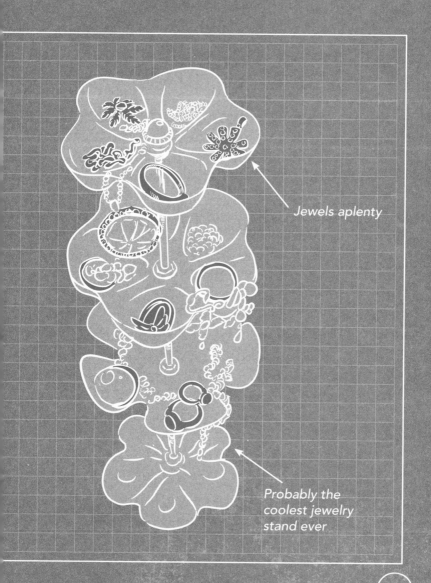

Jewels aplenty

*Probably the
coolest jewelry
stand ever*

SPACE-SAVING SCARF HANGER

Own a scarf for all occasions? I personally have every football team scarf ever made, but you might have something more stylish. If, like me, you have a tiny closet and a large collection, you may have yourself a problem.

A cheap solution involves nothing more than a sturdy coat hanger and a set of shower curtain rings. Put the rings on the hanger and loop your scarfs through the rings. Now your scarfs are in a nice neat line and you can easily find the perfect one to complete your outfit.

Super stylish scarves

Curtain ring

NECKLACE TANGLE PREVENTER

It's so frustrating when my many manly chains get tangled up–it can take hours to untangle them. To stop your gold chains from doing the same, especially when you want to take a few on vacation with you, thread them through a straw. This way they won't tangle and you can go on dazzling others with your fashion accessories.

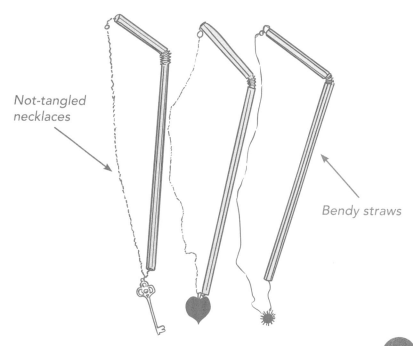

Not-tangled necklaces

Bendy straws

MAKEUP BRUSH HOLDER

If you own a plethora of different-shaped brushes, mainly ones to achieve a completely dust-free face, then you will be in need of this nifty tidy hack. Learning what each of these brushes actually does is hard enough, let alone finding somewhere to store them neatly.

Get a jar or vase, it doesn't matter if it is slightly too tall, and fill it with rice, beads or pebbles. Stick the brushes in (no, not bristles down, silly) handle first, and you have your very own DIY brush holder.

Still-life with brushes

SUNGLASSES RACK

Sometimes, your sunglasses end up everywhere apart from your face–crammed in bags, behind dressers or with friends who never return them. Here is a handy way to keep track of your most trendy shades.

Hammer in a nail in a discreet spot in your bedroom and put up a clothes hanger. Fold your sunnies collection onto the hanger and I guarantee you will notice when a pair goes missing!

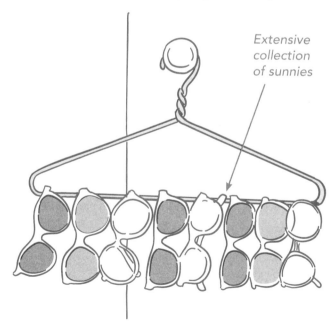

Extensive collection of sunnies

DIY BRACELET RACK

Have you drunk all the wine? Do you need a place to put your large bracelet collection? Perfect!

After draining the last drop, there are actually many uses for that empty bottle. Try shoving on some of your most stylish wrist wear. Wine bottles are tall, so they can fit loads and don't take up much room either. It's a win-win.

Empty wine bottles

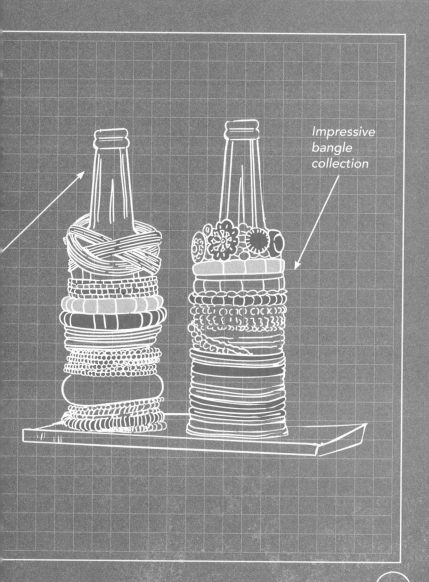

Impressive bangle collection

CLOSET-EXPANSION KIT

I don't know anyone who hasn't suffered the stress and strain of not having enough closet space. Personally, I struggle every day with where to hang my freshly laundered fringe vests. At least, I did until I found this hack.

Save the pull tabs from cans of soft drinks and beer and link them onto the hook of a hanger, letting them rest at the base where the hook meets the hanger itself. You now have created an extra ring to attach another hanger, thus doubling the capacity.

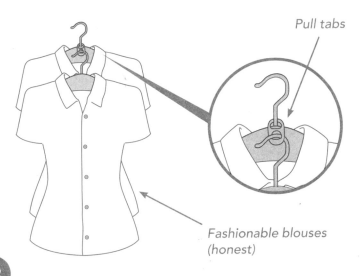

Pull tabs

Fashionable blouses (honest)

VERTICAL CLOTHING

Clothing dilemmas are the worst. You have a perfect image in your head of what you are going to wear, and then you wake up in the morning and fail to find the outfit you were looking for–but you won't settle for anything less than the Hawaiian shirt and the flowing linen trousers. All you can find are velour tracksuits, and on a day like today they just won't do. It is all because of the way you keep your clothes. You know they're in there somewhere, but they just aren't in sight.

Here is a hack to solve this clothing calamity. If you fold your clothes vertically you will be able to see each item clearly and remove them from the drawer without disrupting the rest of the neatly folded piece. How easy is that?

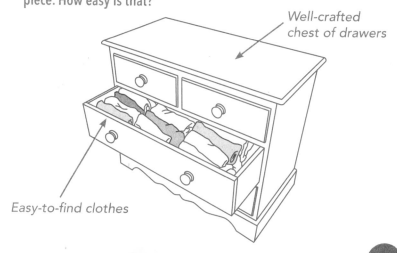

Well-crafted chest of drawers

Easy-to-find clothes

VODKA MATTRESS DISINFECTANT

You know you're sharing your bed with thousands of bacteria every night, don't you? In addition to the pint of sweat we excrete every night, mattresses harbor bacteria, bed bugs, and dust mites. Gross! Obviously, you can't just pop your mattress into the washing machine and give it a quick spin, so what are you supposed to do?

Easy. Raid your drinks cabinet and empty some vodka into a spray bottle. Fill up two-thirds of the bottle and then add a few drops of essential oil. Shake and spray lightly across your mattress. The alcohol will disinfect the mattress, killing any odor-causing bacteria. Just make sure you leave the mattress to air-dry–you don't want your partner to think you have a serious problem.

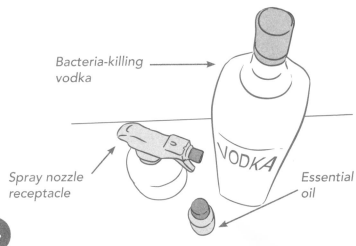

Bacteria-killing vodka

Spray nozzle receptacle

Essential oil

ICE, ICE BEDROOM

If you like to mix things up a little in the bedroom (and yes, I do mean changing the direction of your furniture!), then here's a little trick for getting rid of ugly dents in your carpet.

Simply grab your ice-cube tray, pop a few ice cubes out, and line them up over the indents. Leave them until the cubes have melted. Give the wet area a gentle vacuuming to fluff up the fibers (you can even use a brush or a spoon to help) and the dents are gone–how easy is that?

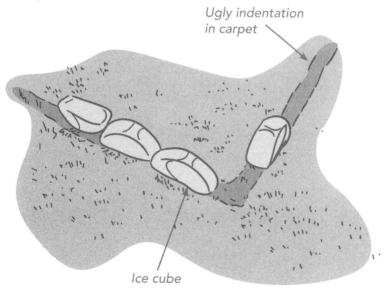

Ugly indentation in carpet

Ice cube

DUVET BURRITO

No, this isn't about eating Mexican food in bed–it's about changing your sheets with ease. Follow these steps:

1. Turn your clean cover inside out and lay it flat on the mattress with the open end at the foot of the bed

2. Lay your duvet on top, making sure the corners line up with the cover

3. Begin to roll the two up, like a burrito, starting from the head of the bed

4. When you get to the end, tuck either end of the burrito into the corners of the cover

5. Unroll the burrito up to the head of the bed and *voilá*, one made bed!

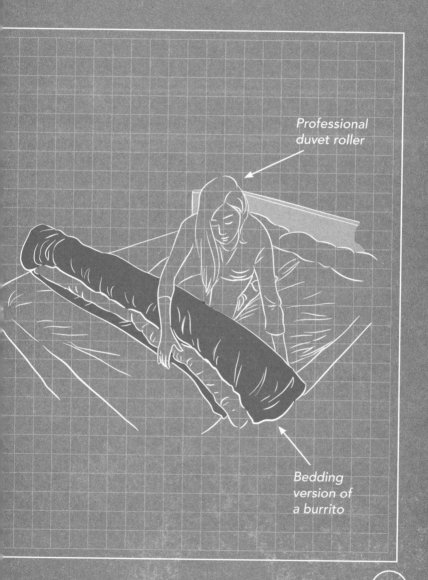

Professional
duvet roller

Bedding
version of
a burrito

SPRAY AWAY

Your bedroom might be the place you go to relax, but it can also be a place where bad smells go to party. Combat nasty odors with this hack.

You will need one tablespoon of vodka (I know, I can hardly believe I'm giving you another hack where booze is being sprayed over things instead of being drunk!), thirty drops of essential oil and six tablespoons of filtered water. Add the alcohol first, then the essential oil and then the filtered water, shake, and spritz around for a sweet-smelling bedroom!

Nearly empty bottle of vodka

Filtered water

VODKA

Various essential oils

SODA WATER STAIN REMOVER

Chips and dip under the duvet might seem like a great idea at the time, but when that hot red salsa ends up on the bedspread (and your lovely cream carpet), it's bad news! Hopefully you will be washing your snack down with a glug of sparkling water, as this will now come in handy for getting rid of the stains.

Pour the fizzy water onto the stain and blot with an absorbent cloth or paper towel (do not rub), and the shameful evidence of your unhygienic eating practices will disappear in no time.

Soda
water

TEABAG WOOD BUFFER

Has your granny ever grimaced when observing you throw a perfectly good (but used) tea bag in the garbage? Well, now you can stick it to her and get that all-important second use out of it!

Boil one quart of water and then add two used tea bags, leave to lightly simmer, and then let the brew cool. Soak a soft cloth in the vat of tea, then prepare to buff your furniture. Wring out the excess liquid and use your cloth to wipe away marks and dirt. Granny will be over the moon.

Tea bag

SQUEEGEE DOG-HAIR REMOVER

If you have a dog, chances are you love the furry oaf–but when your carpet starts to look like a shag rug, courtesy of Fido, it's time to take action. You could try vacuuming the hair up, sure, but the little devils will cling to the carpet for dear life.

Instead, sweep your carpet with a rubber squeegee (or, if you don't have one, rub your hand over the surface while wearing a rubber glove) which will be much more effective. You could even try running an inflated balloon over the surface of your carpet, which will create hair-grabbing static–but if you go for this option, be prepared for some funny looks from your dog. (Go on, admit it; you're itching to try it!)

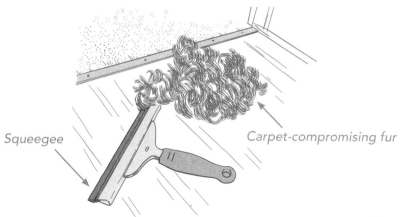

Squeegee

Carpet-compromising fur

MAGIC WATER-RING REMOVER

When your kids (or friends) are more inclined to use your coasters as mini Frisbees than for safeguarding your table from ugly water marks, you're going to have to deal with it. If the worst happens and you end up with a stain, rest assured–your table is not ruined!

Use a hair dryer (set on high) and hold it close to the water mark. Watch it disappear before your very eyes (but don't nod off, as this could take some time). Then rub a little olive oil into the area to moisturize the wood. Now you can sit back with a cuppa and admire your handiwork (but use a coaster!).

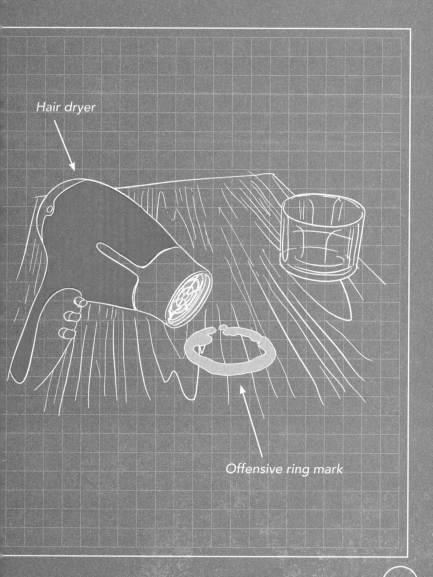

Hair dryer

Offensive ring mark

SMELLY SHOE FRESHENER

I think we can all admit to owning a pair of shoes that stink a little… or a lot, in my case. This handy hint will freshen them up and stop them from stinking up the house.

This a two-pronged hack. One: spray white vinegar over the sneakers, which will help neutralize the odor. Two: get hold of a paper coffee filter, fill it with a small amount of baking soda, and tie up the bundle with a rubber band. Place it in your shoes and wake up in the morning to find your once putrid footwear has stopped smelling like death.

Collection of stinky shoes

DESK HACKS

The desk can often be a dull place. A dull place covered in pens and overshadowed by a dusty-looking screen, among a pile of neon sticky notes. While you are chained to the work station, trying to do something productive with your Wednesday afternoon, the mess is getting to you—so tidy up! Jam jars, toilet-paper-roll tubes, and coffee filters will have you motivated in no time.

JAM JAR PEN HOLDERS

Want to keep pens and stationery in a way that you've never seen before? No? Okay, well, perhaps you just own a lot of pens and pencils and need somewhere to put it all.

Take five large jars, all tall enough for pens to sit comfortably in. For the bottom row, lay three jars on their side in a horizontal row and superglue the jars together. Then glue the other two jars on top. When the jars are dry, you can put your pens, rubber bands, and paper clips inside for a very tidy way to store desk supplies.

Jars having a lie down

Pens and pencils

DESK HACK

If you are a writer or an artist (or just someone with a lot of pens), this hack has your name all over it. (Get it? I made a writing joke!)

To restore order to your desktop, all you need is a shoe box and lots of empty toilet-paper-rolls or tin cans (baked beans removed). Wrap your shoe box in fancy wrapping paper and insert your toilet-paper-rolls or cans so they create lots of individual containers. You now have a fancy-looking desk hack, all the better for helping you write that bestselling novel or draw your way to fame and fortune.

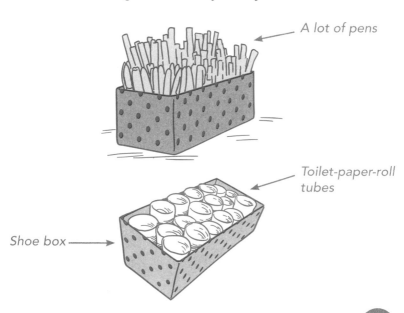

A lot of pens

Toilet-paper-roll tubes

Shoe box

CEREAL BOX DIVIDER

If you've been taking my home office hack advice so far you should now have your game on—but there's always room for improvement. We haven't yet covered your messy drawers. Here's how to do it.

Raid your recycling for a selection of cereal boxes, which will form your drawer dividers—you can cut them to size according to the depth of your drawer (but remember you want to keep the square of the box intact). Cover your boxes in wrapping paper to make them look pretty, then place them upright in your drawers and fill them with your office junk!

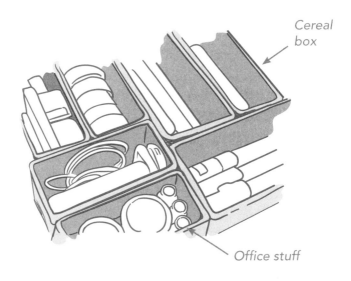

Cereal box

Office stuff

COFFEE FILTER
SCREEN WIPE

As you make your morning cup of java, spare a thought for the humble coffee filter. You may think these little cones of paper are good for nothing other than filtering your morning brew, but they make excellent screen wipes for laptops, tablets, phones, and television screens. Unlike paper towels, filters are lint-free, which makes them much better at picking up dust and cutting static.

Simply spray the coffee filter with a little water, and it will clean your screen without leaving an annoying layer of fluff behind. Coffee filters are super absorbent–also handy when you run out of toilet paper.

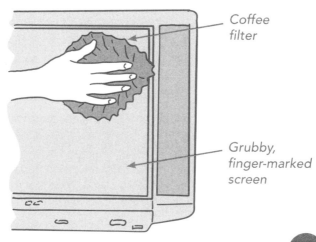

Coffee
filter

Grubby,
finger-marked
screen

DIY MAIL BOARD

Ever find that mail keeps stacking up on your surfaces? It is a common problem in my house and while some of us would throw it all away, others of us appreciate cards and pictures and keep it...all of it. Which means you will need somewhere to display it all.

Get yourself a thick piece of cardboard or even some plywood. To make a padded layer to pin your all-important film-casting offers and self-portraits, use a soft layer of foam and staple it into place. Then cover in fabric, tuck the excess neatly at the back, and fix it in place with staples.

To create a crisscross shape to attach love notes from various models, actors and pop stars, use lengths of ribbon, stretched diagonally across both ways, using tacks where the ribbons cross to hold them in place. Again staple the loose ends onto the back.

Create a hook with a length of leftover ribbon stapled into the two top corners at the back, then bang a nail into the wall and hang it up.

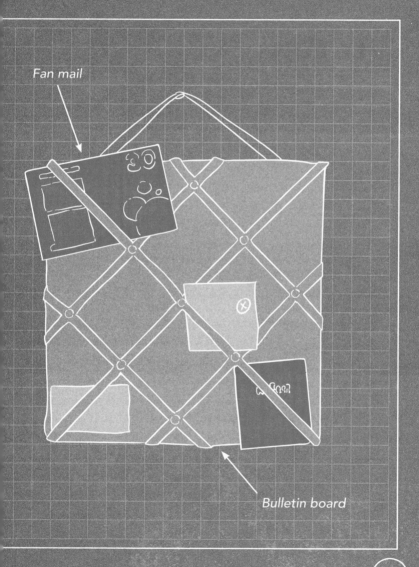

Fan mail

Bulletin board

SMARTPHONE VIDEO-CHAT STAND

Have you reached that confusing stage in life where you actually might be important at work? People in Milan really want to video-call you? Well, if you have and you find yourself holding your phone far too close to your face, giving your caller never-before-seen footage up your nasal passage, then here is a trick to make it look like you know what you're doing.

Take an old cassette case (you may have to visit a vintage shop to find one, or a museum) and turn it inside out so it locks at an angle. Put it down onto your desk and place your phone in the part that is sticking up–they'll never know!

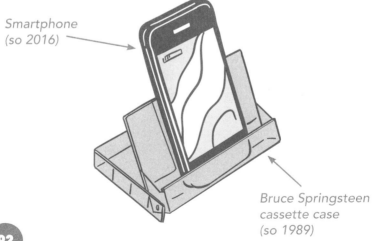

Smartphone (so 2016)

Bruce Springsteen cassette case (so 1989)

LAUNDRY HACKS

It's boring and it's a pain, let's face it. Whether you would just rather be kicking back with a beer or running a marathon, whatever floats your boat, have a go at some of these tidy hacks. They'll speed up the chore and could even make it more fun....Grab some tights for your deodorant stains, and some pool noodles for your clothes horse, and let's whip up a storm in the laundry room.

BEDDING TIDY HACK

My linen closet is best left shut, because when it's opened, it's like an avalanche waiting to happen…and that is never a good thing. Wouldn't it be nice to pull out a sheet and not have everything fall down with it, only to realize that what you were pulling at was the wrong thing anyway?

Here is a clever tip to give you a bit of help. Fold your sheets into the matching pillowcase, and then when it comes to making the bed it won't be such a mountainous task.…Like what I did here?

Pillowcase cleverly concealing a sheet

NO-SLIP HANGERS

Is there anything more annoying than clothes that keep slipping off hangers? There are many things more annoying, but here we're dealing with hangers, so pay attention.

Naughty hangers *can* be transformed into good hangers with the help of rubber bands. Simply wrap a rubber band around the end of your hanger, and your clothes will stay exactly where they are supposed to be, rather than on the floor.

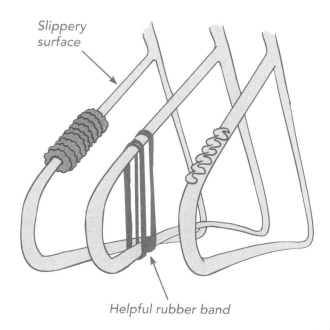

Slippery surface

Helpful rubber band

NO-CREASE NOODLE

Do you dread the thought of ironing your clothes once they've dried? What do you mean you don't know what an iron is?!

Crease-free is the way to be, and here's how to achieve it. If you air-dry your clothes on a horse (no, not an actual horse) they are more likely to crease up. To smooth out the proceedings, cut a pool noodle into bits that match the length of the bars on your clothes rack, slip the noodle bits in place and hang your clothing on top for a more wrinkle-free result.

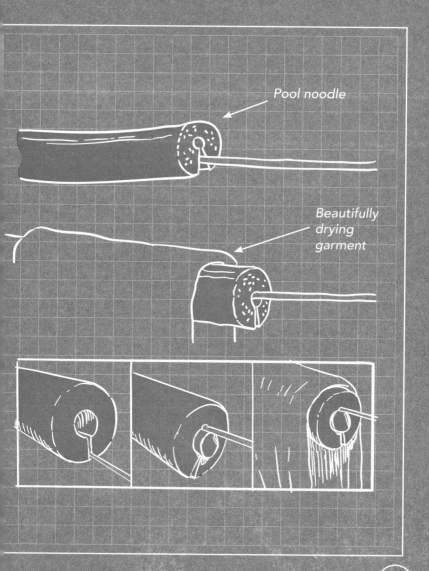

Pool noodle

Beautifully drying garment

DISAPPEARING DEODORANT STAINS

Are deodorant stains plaguing your clothes? They aren't too much of a problem for my fringe vests, but smart T-shirt days can pose a problem. Never fear—women's tights are here!

Here's the way to use them: simply rub the deodorant stain with the tights and the notorious white marks will disappear. Maybe it's something to do with all the tiny holes—who knows? Who cares?

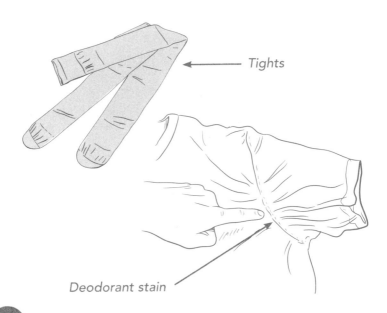

Tights

Deodorant stain

GREASE-STAIN REMOVER

I find myself covered in grease and oil stains frequently–I'm not into cars and engines, I just like the smell. So, with that in mind, here is a handy trick to remove the grimy stains.

Simply crumble chalk over the offending area. (Put enough on there to cover the stain/stains completely.) Leave it like that overnight, and in the morning shake off the chalk to reveal a stain-free piece of clothing.

Chalk can also be used to remove those tougher stains that tend to form around the neck of shirts. Rub the chalk around the neck and leave it for ten minutes. Then wash as you would usually and– ta-da!–stain is gone!

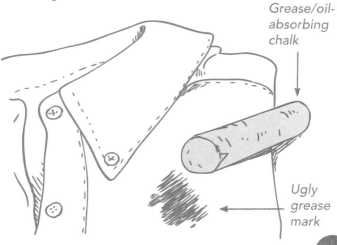

Grease/oil-absorbing chalk

Ugly grease mark

DIY DRYER SHEETS

Don't fork out for expensive dryer sheets—make your own!

Use up all your old towels and sheets for this, cutting them up into small rectangles. Then find a large glass jar, and add to it half a glass of white vinegar (yes, it smells a bit funny, but it has fabric-softening properties!) and then add fifteen drops of an essential oil (make it a nice one). Then soak your rectangles in the jar, the longer the better. When you are ready to use them, wring out the liquid and place one per wash in the dryer. Your clothes will come out smelling fresh and fragrant.

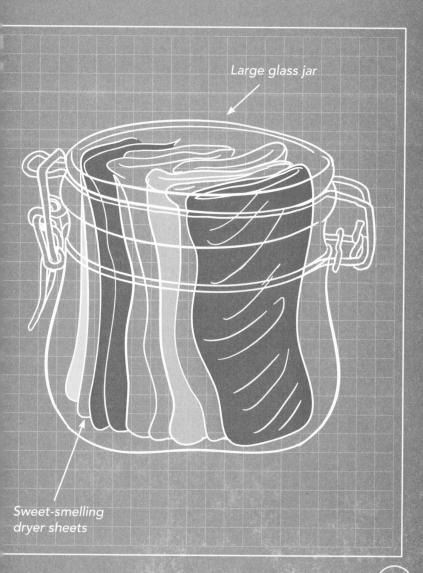

Large glass jar

Sweet-smelling
dryer sheets

NO-BRAINER IRONING BOARD KEEPER

If you're the kind of dummy who stores the ironing board in a packed closet, getting it out each time you need it will involve an infuriating tug of war. Luckily for you, we have a simple hack that will free up some closet space *and* lower your blood pressure.

Simply nail two coat hooks on a wall or the back of a door—yes, it's that easy! You can then hang your ironing board out of the way until it's needed. Even a DIY dufus can cope with this one.

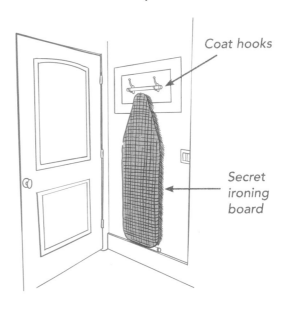

Coat hooks

Secret ironing board

ODD SOCKS

Odd socks–need I say more? Where do they go in the washing machine? Do they disappear into a black hole? Are they teleported to another universe? Stop this nonsense and invest in a mesh bag. Pop your socks inside, place the bag in the washing machine and I can guarantee that the same number of socks will be there when you take the bag out again. Better yet, give everyone in your family their own mesh laundry bag–no more sock sorting. Hooray!

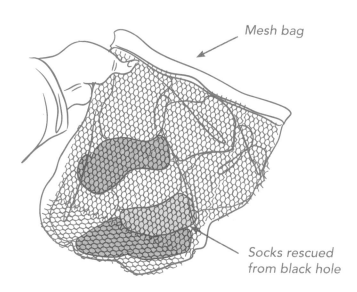

Mesh bag

Socks rescued from black hole

GRASS-STAIN REMEDY

Whether you are an adventurous child, a keen gardener, or anyone who spends a lot of time in grassy areas, you will have come across the infamous grass stain. Most definitely you will be in need of a grass-stain-remover recipe.

Take one glass of water. The size of the glass will depend on how concentrated you want the mixture to be and how many grass stains you find on your clothing. You will need equal parts of ammonia, good washing detergent, and white vinegar. Put it all in an empty clean spray bottle and give it a good shake. Then, just spray it on the offending mark and rub it right off.

Spray bottle

Grass-stained trousers

CARDBOARD CUTOUTS

Folding is quite possibly the dullest part of your laundry routine. It can often end with a hurling motion, followed in quick succession by the "shut the drawer and hope never to open it again" technique. The next morning arrives, however, and there is no way you are finding that clean vest you swore you washed yesterday. This is a more creative, fun way to fold!

Take a large piece of flat cardboard, and we all have one of those in the shed or loft, and fold one piece of clothing to the width you want all your clothes to be. Draw lines down each side and fold the cardboard along each line. Then cut about halfway up the lines, vertically. Lay a T-shirt or top on the cardboard, flip up each side and then finally flip up the cutout section at the bottom. See! In three easy motions you have the perfectly folded top.

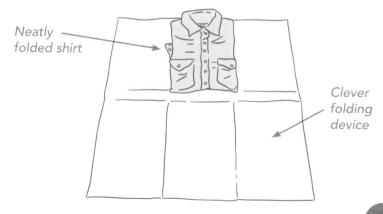

Neatly folded shirt

Clever folding device

GENERAL HOUSEHOLD HACKS

Here we have some super-useful hacks that you might never need for the household, but we thought we'd pop them in anyway. You never know when you might come across a few fragile Christmas decorations that need saving, or some deadly wrapping paper tubes ready to trip you up....But it does happen, so we've covered it.

CABLE CASES

Is your house starting to resemble a tightrope-walking competition? Phone chargers, computer cables, and USB cords are the worst culprits to turn your living room, bedroom, and kitchen into lethal tripping zones. Even when you make the effort to unplug them and bundle them all up in a drawer, somehow twenty or so cables transform into one giant terrifying knot, making it impossible to use without a game of tug of war.

To stop this right away, fold each electrical cord lengthways and slide it into a toilet-paper-roll tube. This way all the cords are separated, easy to use, and can be kept neat and tidy.

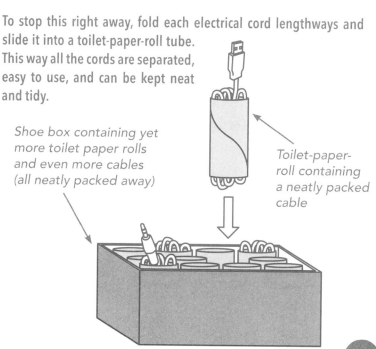

Shoe box containing yet more toilet paper rolls and even more cables (all neatly packed away)

Toilet-paper-roll containing a neatly packed cable

BINDER CLIP CABLES

Some cords, like those for your computer or television, can't be put away so easily. So instead of having them hanging down and lying on the floor, fasten them to a desk or cabinet with a binder clip. Trap the wires into the clip section and then put a tack through one of the clip arms and fix it in place. Push the other arm down to lie flat and there's your quick way to tidy cables.

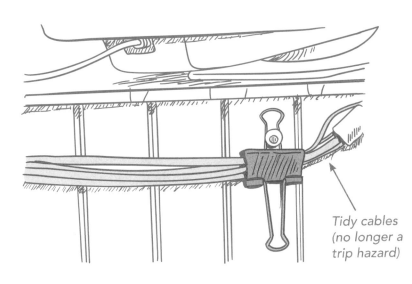

Tidy cables
(no longer a
trip hazard)

ABOVE-THE-DOOR STORAGE

If you're short like me, then you may have neglected to utilize the space above you. When tidying, always remember to look up. You will be surprised by what you will find all the way up there…. Although let's hope there aren't any giant spiders lurking around.

Install a wooden shelf or plank above a doorway, and like magic you have created some extra space for the things that you won't need every day but will need every so often. It's simple but effective!

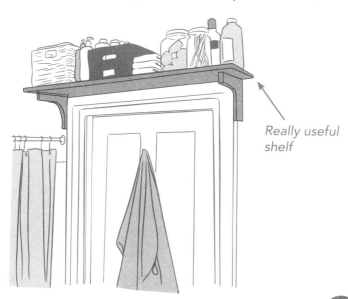

Really useful shelf

PHONE CHARGE CADDY

Being glued to a phone is a typical thing these days and the more the phones are glued to faces the more they need charging. This DIY phone charger case is bound to come in handy and will prevent the all-important mobile phone from being left to charge on the floor or surface—here's how to make it.

Use a large empty lotion or shampoo bottle and draw the outline of your phone onto the outside—straight line at the front, rising up to a higher line at the back. Then cut along the line you've just drawn with scissors. On the higher side cut a hole big enough for the plug to sit in. Once you have your holder cut out, sand down the surfaces to get rid of any writing or logos on the bottle and to make an easier surface to stick decorative material. Use glue to cover the outside with fabric (remember to make a hole for the plug in the fabric and to tidy up the edges). Once it's dry, you are ready to use the DIY phone charging case.

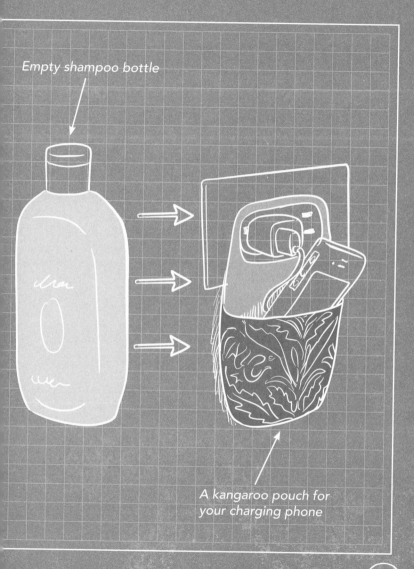

Empty shampoo bottle

A kangaroo pouch for your charging phone

EGG CARTON STORAGE

Here is a really quick tidy hack for putting away holiday decorations. Egg boxes! If they keep your fragile eggs safe, they will definitely protect your fragile baubles. If you want to be extra careful, line the egg box with bubble wrap.

Egg carton

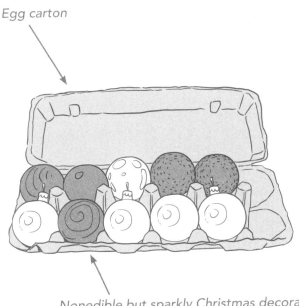

Nonedible but sparkly Christmas decorations

CUPCAKE PAN ORGANIZER

Are you sick of muffins and small cakes? Or just had enough of making them yourself? Well, here is another use for cupcake tin molds. They come in really handy if you need more compartments in drawers. They can be used in the home office, kitchen, or bedroom; you name it the cupcake pan will adapt. Fill it with what you like: keys, mini notepads, tape measures, or even some tooth-rotting sweets.

All the things you keep losing in one place

SHOE BOX STORAGE

There is no point in buying drawer compartments or dividers when you have cardboard shoe boxes lying around. If you have recently been on a crazy shoe-shopping spree, you may find that you have rather a lot. Instead of chucking them, use them as space dividers in your larger desk drawers and even your clothing drawers. Paint them, or cover the boxes in bright wrapping paper, and fill: sort out your DVD collection, books, photo albums, CDs, electrical items, etc. Or use them to vertically sort your T-shirts, sweaters, and trousers. Put the lid back on and slide the drawer closed. Being tidy has never been so simple.

Beautifully folded T-shirts

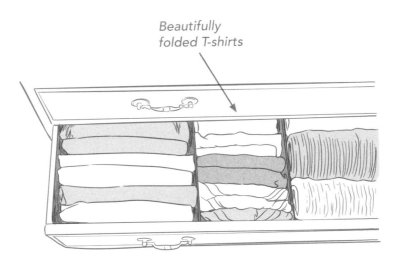

SHUTTER SPACE

If you find an old shutter deep in the garage, your first thought shouldn't be to burn it.

It could be used for cheap firewood…or how about a letter filer? Bet you hadn't thought of that one! So, paint it a nice color and hang it in your home office or kitchen. Even if you don't open the letters, because we all know they aren't likely to be fan mail, it will eliminate the pile of dreaded letters.

Touching family photograph

Window shutter

EARPHONE HACK

I find that locating earphones is a terrible problem. Once they're thrown into my bag, it is difficult to see where they might be hiding. When finally discovered, unearthing the buggers can be tricky; they latch on to books, water bottles, lunch boxes, pretty much anything, and I find myself on the train ripping out the wire frantically along with the contents of the bag. No one wants the insides of your bag hurled through space at them during their morning commute. For a smoother, more stylish way of removing your earphones, follow this tidy hack.

You will need two clothespins, a tube of superglue, the headphones, of course, and perhaps some paint or colored pens if you would like to decorate them. First step is to decorate; a diplomatic luminous shade will do. When dry, superglue the two longest sides together, making sure they are top to tail. Trap the jack into the bottom and wind the cable around the other side. Close the pins and you have a great way of storing your earphones.

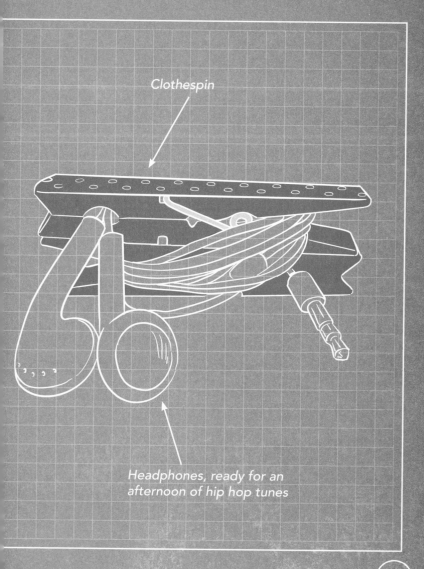

Clothespin

Headphones, ready for an
afternoon of hip hop tunes

WRAP-UP HACK

Year-round falling over a wrapping paper tube is a common hazard. What with all these events: birthdays, Christmas…just lethal. They are silent rollers that can often creep up on you, catching you unawares and taking you out when you least expect it.

However, there is no need to panic. I have found that securing them in a wardrobe bag and hanging them in a closet keeps them locked away and off the floors!

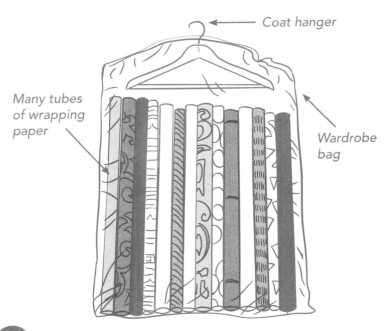

Coat hanger

Many tubes of wrapping paper

Wardrobe bag

BUNGEE SHELF

Don't settle for a boring old shelf, make a bungee one! You can hang up sunglasses, scarves, wiry electrical items, jewelry, and whatever else suits your fancy; also, it looks cool.

All you need is a bungee, a length of wooden board, superglue, a drill, wire, and a hook (to hang the shelf with when finished). Begin by drilling two holes, one at each end of the wooden board. Remember to make these holes small so the bungee holds tightly, and then dip the end of the bungee cord into the superglue and quickly (and carefully) thread it into the hole. Using a picture-hanging kit is probably the easiest way to hang the shelf. Now you too can have a trendy bungee shelf.

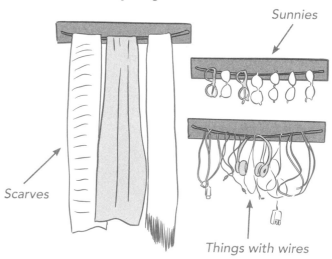

Sunnies

Scarves

Things with wires

TWINKLING LIGHTS UP

No more will the month of December be spent disentangling Christmas lights. By looping the wires around coat hangers they will stay knot-free all year round until their unveiling on the tree. You can also hang them up so that they don't get bashed around and are easy to find when you do finally use them; happy decorating!

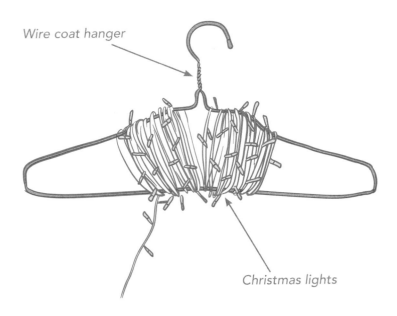

Wire coat hanger

Christmas lights

STICK-'EM-UP REMOTES

Do you struggle to find the remote, wasting perfectly good television time asking family members to please get up from the sofa to look for the remote? Let's face it, it's a common danger in the living room, but after reading this hack, it will be a distant memory.

Nominate an area (the side of the TV cabinet or somewhere of equal surface area) to keep the game controllers and television remotes, then use Velcro to fix them in place. All you have to do is remember to stick them back.

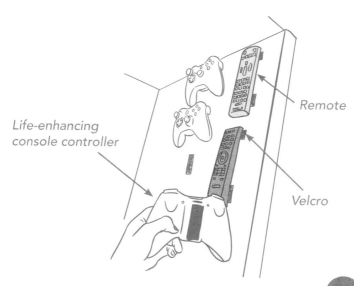

Remote

Life-enhancing
console controller

Velcro

COLOR-CODED KEYS

I'm not sure how this has happened but I appear to have more keys than my kids' school janitor. I spend hours juggling my key ring trying to find the right key before I can get into my home, office, man shed, etc. Luckily, there's an old-fashioned solution—paint your keys with colored nail polish. This way you should easily be able to pick out the right key for the right keyhole. Personally, I favor a discreet dot at the top of the key, but knock yourself out—paint the entire key head neon or add some stripes. Works like a charm! (Not so helpful if you can't remember what the pink key is used for of course, but it shouldn't take long for you to get used to which color means which door.

"What were you thinking?"
nail polish

How many keys do you need?

LEATHER SCUFF ERASER

Ever thought a banana could help with the scuffs on your shoes? Well, it's not as strange as you might think. Potassium, which is found in bananas, is also found in shoe polish! So potassium, plus the natural oils in the fruit's skin, equals a great boot buffer.

Be sure to use slightly green bananas, as there will be fewer banana bits to come off on your shoes. Simply take your scuffed shoe and rub the pithy side of the skin all over it. The banana skin will take away the marks and leave you with some pretty shiny footwear.

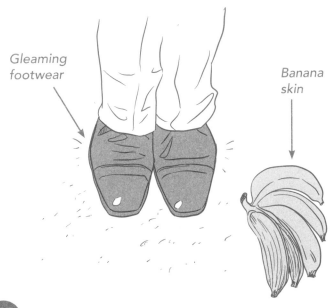

Gleaming footwear

Banana skin

GARDEN HACKS

Help in the garden is always welcome, and when it comes to asking for a bit of help, most people you know suddenly disappear without a trace. That's where these garden tidy hacks come in. From quick and easy recipes for fertilizer to transportation devices so that you can show off your best tulips, consider this your new gardening companion.

BAKING SODA WEED KILLER

For those of us who covet a pristine patio or driveway, weeds are the stuff of nightmares. And if you have them bad, you'll stop at nothing short of detonating a nuclear warhead to make sure they don't come back.

But there is a less apocalyptic way to clear your driveway: pour a thick layer of baking soda into the cracks where the weeds rear their ugly heads. Sodium has the effect of drying out plant foliage, which means those dastardly dandelions will be a thing of the past.

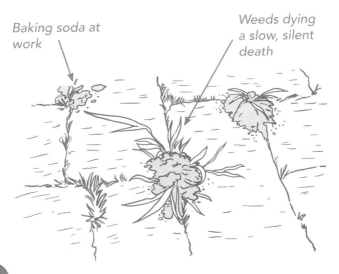

Baking soda at work

Weeds dying a slow, silent death

HOSE STAND

There's nothing worse than a nasty kink in the garden hose. You bend down to disentangle it, lose control of the end, and get a face full of cold water. To keep your hose in a kink-free state make sure you keep it on its very own bucket stand. Use a galvanized paint bucket and drill three holes into the bottom, in a triangle shape. Screw the end of the bucket onto the side of your shed and wrap your hose neatly around the outside of it; you could even sit your sprinkler inside of the bucket. Your hose will be neat and tidy, and most important, knot-free!

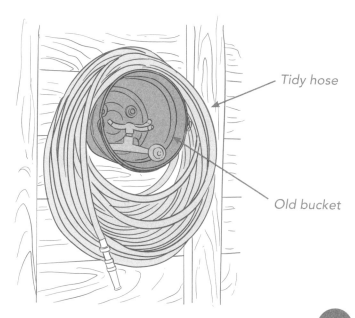

Tidy hose

Old bucket

TWINE DISPENSER

The sunflowers are in the ground, swaying in the breeze. You reach for the twine in the shed and after yanking away at the ball, still no loose end. What a disaster.

For a simple but effective twine dispenser, put your ball of string into a funnel and pull the loose end through the hole; it will glide easily. To make this even niftier, hammer a nail through the top of the funnel near to the lip, then attach the nail into the side of your shed, pop your ball of twine back into the top and feed the string through. You'll be the trendsetter on your block in no time.

Funnels —

Twine —

MILK BOTTLE CADDY

If you have ever gotten to the bottom of the vegetable garden and have realized that you have left the pruners in the shed, then you will feel my pain. No one wants to spend the day trudging what feels like miles back and forth up the garden, forgetting one tool at a time! So carrying your garden essentials around is vital.

I have one of these wire milk bottle caddies; it works as a great way of keeping your day-to-day garden things all in one place, ready to pick up and take out into the garden with you whenever you need.

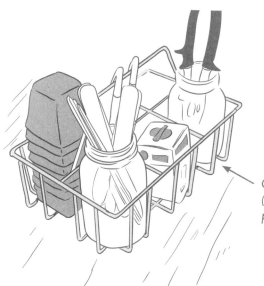

Garden helper (shame it can't pour a G&T)

CHICKEN FEEDER SHELF

This hack will help in the event of a clutter catastrophe. "Is there really no more room for my vegetable-growing manuals and tomato-shining equipment?" I hear you call. Well, never fear, here's what to do. Make a friend who keeps chickens and steal one of his chicken feeders–or ask politely, your choice. These trough-like feeders come in really handy in the garden shed. You'll need as much surface space as possible for seedlings and potting, so having lots of shelving and storage is essential.

Seed packets

Your friend's chicken feeder

GARDEN PEGBOARD

Is your shed looking a little like a bomb has hit it, with tools everywhere and tangled twine and packets of seeds strewn about? Don't worry, I've got a tidy solution! Your shed will no longer look like it belongs to a hoarder gone wrong.

Pegboards are your answer! Put them in the shed or designated garden area and paint them. Hang up all your garden equipment and leave all your surfaces free for potting.

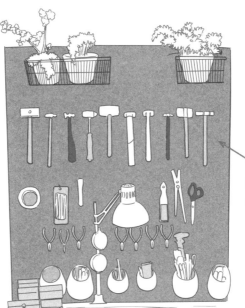

Pleasing display of tools

BUNGEE HOLDALL

Gardening can sometimes seem like you are starring in your very own slapstick comedy–stepping on to the end of the rake you didn't know was there, only for it to whack you square in the face, sending you stumbling blindly into the beanpoles, before jamming your foot into the watering can.

For a shed free from danger, use bungee rope hooks to secure your most lethal rake and most menacing poles. Hammer in hooks on either side of where you would like your tools to stand, attach the bungee hooks, and keep the accidents at bay.

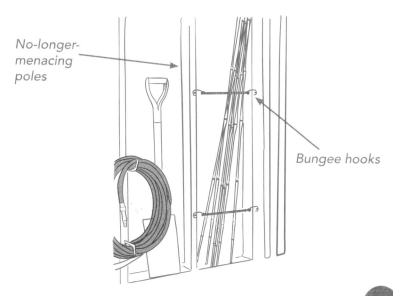

No-longer-menacing poles

Bungee hooks

SEEDY TAPE

When planting seeds, it's important to get the spacing right, but this can be awkward when scattering tiny dark specks onto soil.

A toilet-paper roll is your answer. Lay a length of tissue down and spray with water until damp. As you place the seeds central along the strip you will be able to see where they land. and thus space them evenly. When that's done, starting along the long edge, fold a third of the paper over, then fold the other third over to cover the seeds. Spray again with water so the paper sticks and carry out into the garden.

Make shallow furrows in the garden and place your toilet-paper roll in them. Cover in soil and you have yourself the perfect garden.

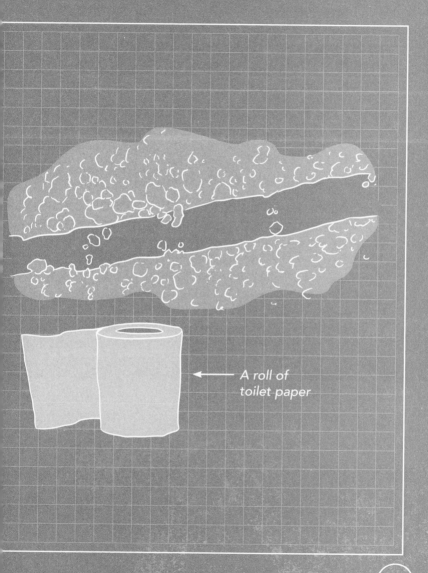

A roll of
toilet paper

135

SEED JARS

I've never planted all of the marigold seeds inside the packets, nor the tomatoes or runners; I'd live in more of a jungle than a garden if I did! To make sure leftover seeds don't get lost, so you can use them next year, assign them a jar to live in over the winter months. This way they will be all in one place and they will be tucked away safe and sound!

Airtight container

Next year's tomatoes

SEED ALBUMS

It might seem a little strange for your friends to open up your family photo album and find treasured packets of seeds instead... but photo albums do make excellent seed organizers.

Slip the packets into the plastic compartments when you have seeds leftover and you are finished planting. That way they are organized, all in one place, ready for another day of gardening. Perhaps keep the album safe in the shed so it doesn't get mixed up with the family photo albums.

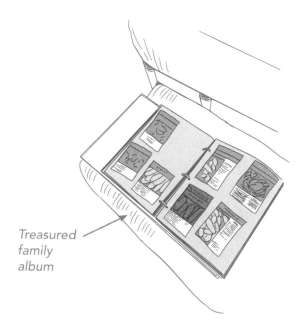

Treasured family album

TWO-FOR-ONE HERBS

Supermarket herbs are not designed to last–that's why they keel over the second you walk through your front door. Instead of giving the supermarkets more of your hard-earned money, try this: split your potted herb in two and plant in good potting compost in individual containers. Most herbs die early because there are too many plants crammed into one pot. Give them space to breathe and you should prolong their life span and get double the herbs for your money. Even better, grow your own herbs from seed (I'll have to stick to supermarket ones; our family's green thumb skipped a generation with me).

Shrubbus maximus (again, not the real name)

Herbus delicius (not the actual Latin name)

TOILET-PAPER-ROLL PLANTERS

Your toilet-paper-roll tube not only faithfully holds your toilet tissue but can also be brought out into the greenhouse with you too, for the purposes of planting.

Cut the cardboard tube in half (across its diameter) for two makeshift seedling pots. Then cut four even slits and fold to form the base of your planter, making sure there's a small, square hole for good drainage. Fill the clever pots with soil and a seed and watch them come to life for half the price.

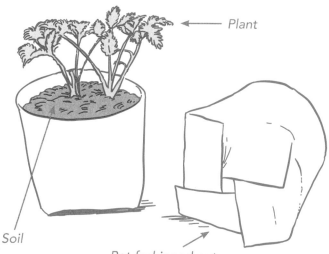

Plant

Soil

Pot fashioned out of a toilet-paper-roll tube

PITHY PLANTERS

When life gives you lemons, squeeze them and keep their rinds for more planters!

Once you have squeezed your lemons, scrape the pulp out using a spoon, down to the white pith. Pierce a small hole or three in the bottom for drainage. Fill it with soil and one or two seeds. Water them, put them in a window or greenhouse and wait.

Give it a few weeks until the plants have started sprouting. And here's where rotting fruit becomes our friend: plant the seedling, lemon and all, in your garden. The plant will grow and the lemon will rot and nourish the soil, helping your seedling in more than one way!

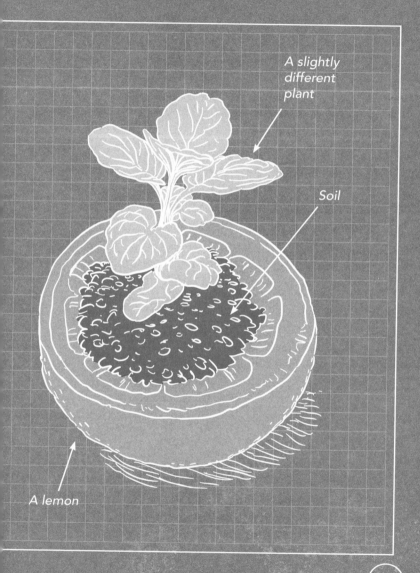

A slightly
different
plant

Soil

A lemon

COFFEE COMPOST

It's hard to believe that used coffee grounds have a function other than filling your garbage can, but they do! They can help your garden grow.

There's a long "sciencey" explanation for this, so let's do it in short: the grounds can help improve soil structure because they are pH neutral, and evidence suggests that they repel slugs and snails. You can put it on the compost heap or add it straight to your plants with some fertilizer.

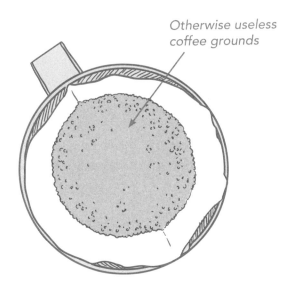

Otherwise useless coffee grounds

GARDEN-TOOL RUST REMOVER

At some point, your favorite hedge trimmers are going to get rusty. I know, it's a traumatizing thought, but it's a reality. Get a grip.

If the worst happens and you are faced with rusty blades, get the car polish out, blot some on a cloth, rub into the oxidized edges, and they'll soon be shiny and new and ready for action!

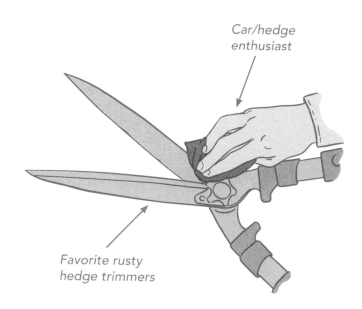

Car/hedge
enthusiast

Favorite rusty
hedge trimmers

SAND STORAGE FOR TOOLS

There are three good reasons to keep a bucket of sand in your garden: 1) you can sit in your deck chair sipping a margarita, pretending you're on vacation in the Bahamas, 2) your kid can use it to play in, and 3) you can store your garden tools in the sand to stop them from rusting.

Simply fill a container with builder's sand (note: avoid a trip to the beach, as salt and metal don't mix) and "plant" your garden tools in it, with the handles sticking up. The sand will protect against rust and corrosion; also, as sand is abrasive, it will help to keep your tools clean and sharp–you dig?

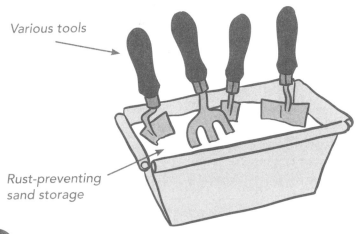

Various tools

Rust-preventing sand storage

TOOL CADDY

So golf wasn't really your game? Some say it's a good walk spoiled anyway.

Don't worry about wasting all that expensive equipment you bought–sell the clubs and use your flashy golf bag to transport your essential garden tools, for an easy way to carry your rakes, spades, and hoes along with you down the green–I mean, garden.

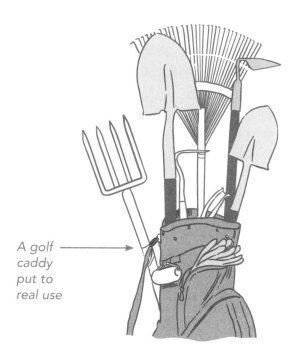

A golf caddy put to real use

BANANA FERTILIZER

Who would have guessed that roses like bananas too? Well, they do! But only the peel. It works great as a makeshift fertilizer.

Cut the peel into one-inch strips, lengthwise, and bury in the soil just beneath the base of your rose plant. Do this once every month. The potassium in the banana skin feeds the rose plant and helps to prevent disease. Your roses will thank you for it!

Flourishing
roses

Some
soil

Banana skin

MARBLE VASES

This hack is really not as sophisticated as it sounds. It's a basic way to help your cut flowers sit upright in your vase.

To achieve the desired effect, simply throw some marbles into the bottom of your vase before you begin arranging the stems. It'll help the tulips stay rooted down below the surface of the water and make flower arranging child's play. A bit like marbles–get it?!

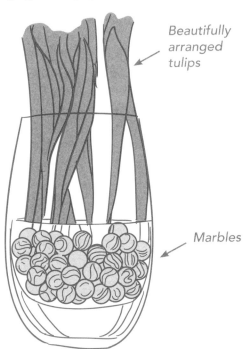

Beautifully arranged tulips

Marbles

BALLOON TRAVEL VASE

Picture the scene–your finest parrot tulips are in bloom and you want to cut a few and swing by your friend Steve's house to gloat about your horticultural success. But Steve lives twenty minutes away, which means the picture-perfect tulips might droop a little and spoil the effect. Don't worry, here is a perfect solution.

Find a balloon, fill to about a quarter of the way with water and stick your freshly cut darlings in. The rubber balloon should tighten around the stems just enough to seal your new travel vase and stop any spillage. Now you can really stick it to Steve.

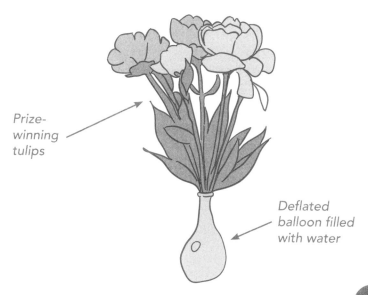

Prize-winning tulips

Deflated balloon filled with water

KIDS'
HACKS

Kids are delightful…until they start making a mess and then they don't seem so cute. Days off and family holidays begin in a happy mood until ice cream is splattered down the front of T-shirts and painting takes a turn for the worse when the walls become the work of art. To return to blissful days again, I've got a few handy hacks up my sleeve.

MESS-FREE PAINTING

This next hack is great for when you want to do some painting with your kid but can't face clearing up afterwards. Let's be honest: kids + paint = domestic Armageddon.

Squirt some paint into a sealable bag (the large kind you use for freezing food) and tape the bag to a window, making sure it's well sealed. Your child can then create a masterpiece with their hands, and you can put your feet up and admire their handiwork. This hack is fun, educational, creative, *and* mess-free! What's not to love?

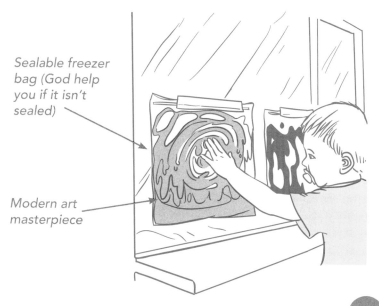

Sealable freezer bag (God help you if it isn't sealed)

Modern art masterpiece

ICE POP-DRIP CATCHERS

Use cupcake liners to catch the drips from your kid's delicious ice pop. Simply poke the ice pop stick down through the middle of an upturned cupcake liner to create a little cup that will catch the offending drips. Now, if only there were a hack to combat brain freeze....

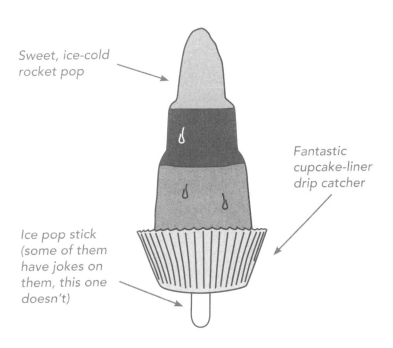

Sweet, ice-cold rocket pop

Fantastic cupcake-liner drip catcher

Ice pop stick (some of them have jokes on them, this one doesn't)

CRAYON REMOVER

Crayon scribbles on the wall are the bane of any household with young children. But this way of removing them (the scribbles, not the kids) will put your mind at ease.

Take a cloth, spray a little water-displacing lubricant on it (the kind that comes in a bold blue-and-yellow can) and apply to the offending area. The crayon marks will magically disappear!

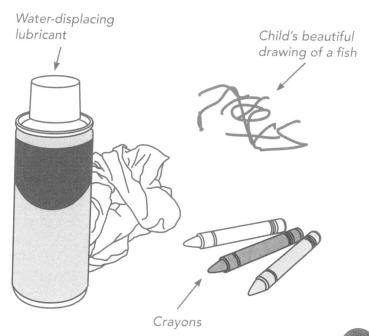

Water-displacing lubricant

Child's beautiful drawing of a fish

Crayons

DISHWASHER ART RACK

Darn it! The dishwasher has blown up. "How on earth will we ever wash the plates?" you cry. Well, clean dishes are out of the question for a while.... However, if you are looking to store art equipment, think yourself very lucky indeed. Your children are probably budding artists– Salvador Dalís in the making, or that is what you interpreted when they showed you a picture of Grandma melting over what looked like molten lava in space....

Use the slots where plates once were to put coloring books and folders of fine art. Use the silverware holder to store pens, pencils, and paintbrushes. The kids will now have all they need to flourish artistically.

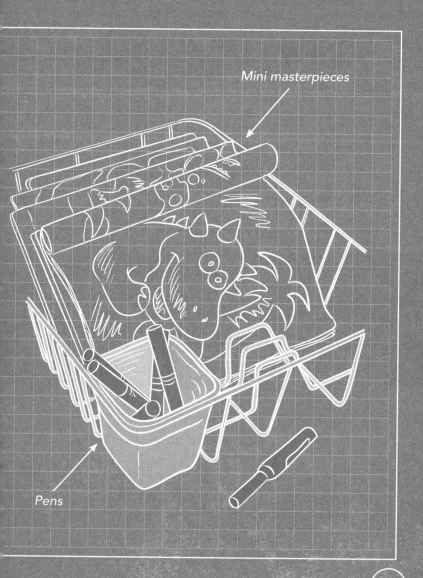

Mini masterpieces

Pens

VELCRO TOY STORAGE

Panda and bunny, bear and mutant caterpillar have reached an age now where they are still lovable but perhaps just tend to take up room, getting dusty on the bed or on the floor. Forbidden from being thrown away, there needs to be a way of keeping them, but in a tidy way. "Is it really possible?" you ask. Yes, it is, and this hack will be the lifesaver in the children's bedroom.

Stick a piece of Velcro to the wall. Make sure it is the rougher side and then stick on the fluffy toys. Suspended quite comfortably on the wall, panda, bunny, bear, and mutant caterpillar will actually look tidy...unbelievable.

Favorite toys

Velcro strip

GLUE SPONGE

Arts and crafts with children can often get very messy. Somehow even when just one gold star needs to be glued onto the page, kids will use half a bottle of glue just in case the star decided to rip itself off the page, using its own raw strength. The rest of the bottle will have ended up lid off, on the floor, found hours later underneath the table, dried onto the floorboards.

So sometimes you need to have a clever trick up your sleeve to protect the house, the furniture, and the glue supply! Take a small Tupperware box and cut a sponge to fit inside. Then cover the sponge in glue and let it get soaked up. Put the sticky sponge box onto the table. When you need to glue something down, press it onto the sponge and stick it to the page. After arts and crafts are finally over, put the lid back on and keep for the next time.

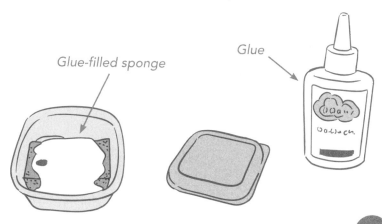

Glue-filled sponge

Glue

MULTIPLE-USE HACKS

Believe it or not, magnetic strips and wine racks are vital ingredients in the art of being tidy. They can be used pretty much anywhere and for anything. Garden shed, kitchen, bathroom, you name it, these things will work anywhere. Here are some great examples of how to use them....

HAIR GRIP STRIP

This one's great for the bathroom. When fashioning my comb-over I like to use bobby pins to complete my look. While holding the strands in position, I reach for the hair pins, but where have they gone? In a fluster I lose my ideal pelt position and overturn absolutely everything in the bathroom, usually yelling as I go. So for the perfect hairstyle in seconds, go to your local DIY shop and get yourself a magnetic strip roll (the kind with a magnet on one side and a sticky surface on the other). Fasten it to the inside of your bathroom cabinet and pin up all of your bobby pins. Trust me, you'll never have a bad hair day again. You can also use it for tweezers and nail clippers, to deal with the mono brow and the yellow toenails.

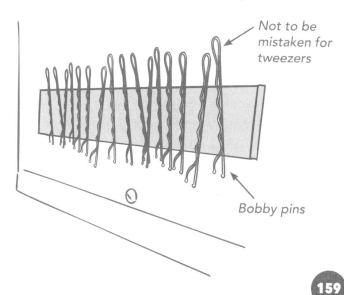

Not to be mistaken for tweezers

Bobby pins

MAGNETS FOR KNIVES

At some point or other in life many of us start to fancy ourselves as professional chefs. The toasted sandwiches have reached new levels; the boundaries of baked beans on toast have been surpassed with Gorgonzola cheese. (The kids didn't like it, but what do they know.) If this is the case for you, you may be rather proud of your kitchen knife set, so why not have them on display? You will need:

1 old wooden board (approximately 16 in x 4 in)
A bit of sandpaper
Power drill
A 1-inch Forstner bit (it should come in your drill bit set)
Fifty-four 1-inch round magnets
Superglue
Two 2½-inch wall-mounting screws

Start by sanding the board down for a softer surface and to remove sharp edges. The goal now is to drill two central lines of nine magnet holes. Remember you are not drilling all the way through–make sure there is space at each end to screw the board into the wall and most importantly to clamp the board down securely.

Superglue two or three round magnets together and then glue them into holes. Finally screw the knife rack onto the kitchen wall, somewhere high up away from the kids.

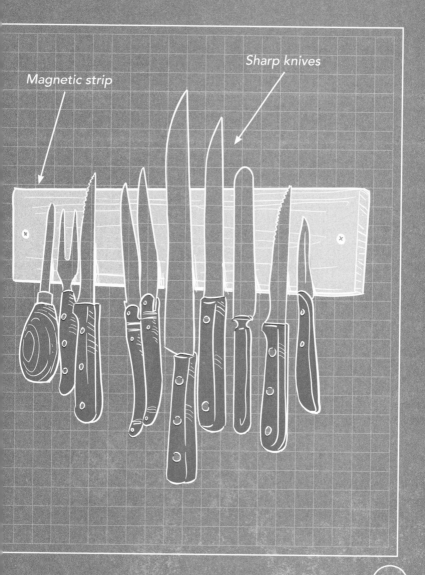

Magnetic strip

Sharp knives

MAKEUP MAGNETS

My shimmery nude palettes far outweigh the amount of containers I own to put them in. That said, they also far outweigh the amount of manly items I own. My mornings can be pretty stressful choosing which shade brings out the auburn hues of my facial hair. So I have come up with a new tidy way to organize my makeup so that I can see what I am working with.

Use an old frame and instead of putting a picture inside, put in a sheet of thin magnetic metal (you can get these from DIY shops). You can cover the metal in wrapping paper or any patterned paper too, to give it a bit of pizzazz. Stick mini magnets onto the makeup you want to stick into the frame. Then put it up in your bedroom or bathroom for a tidier makeup collection.

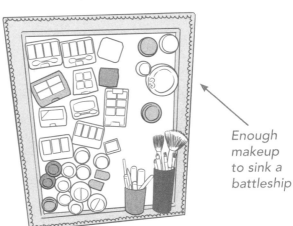

Enough makeup to sink a battleship

SPICE MAGNET

Ooh la la, a spice magnet! No, fortunately you have not turned the page in another book about spicy magnetism; we are still talking about tidying. Phew! Specifically I am talking about putting your spices and herbs into small jars with metal lids. Once again, get your magnetic strip out, this time in the kitchen, and attach it either inside or outside the spice cupboard. Make sure you stick labels on to the bottom of each jar stating what each one is (you don't want the nutmeg mixed up with the garam masala–it might not be the nicest cake you have ever made). Screw the lids on and watch the spice jars dangle enticingly from the magnetic strip. Now you have really spiced up the spice rack.

Grandma's secret spice mix

SHED MAGNETS

Grab your trusty magnets, because, that's right, they can be translated for use in the garden shed too, thanks to the little metal band that hold your brush's bristles in place. You can use an inexpensive roll of magnetic strip and stick a strip on the shed wall. Or you could invest your time in making a paintbrush board using the same method as the kitchen knife board. Then you just have to stick on your (clean) paintbrushes, bristles down, for a tidier shed.

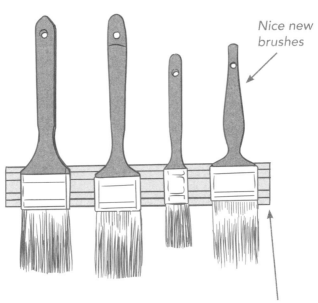

Nice new brushes

The ubiquitous magnetic strip

WINO TOWEL RACK

Wine racks are perfect for storing rolled-up towels, in all shapes and sizes. The towels look shipshape and although your wine rack is now filled with fluffy towels, at least you'll be warm and dry in a neat and tidy fashion. Who needs to be drunk when you've got that?

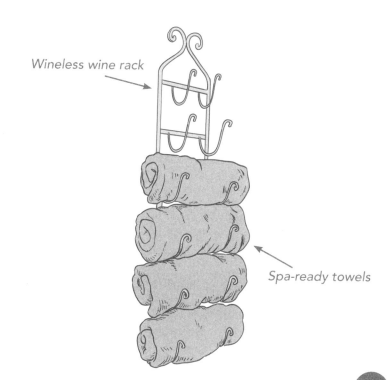

Wineless wine rack

Spa-ready towels

ART-EQUIPMENT RACK

This might seem like a complete waste of a wine rack, but if you have recently upgraded your booze display you can use the old one as an ingenious way to organize your pens and pencils.

Put a glass or plastic cup where a wine bottle would have once sat and slide your pens in. You could even let your inner artist out and color coordinate... perhaps save your street cred for another day.

Pens and pencils

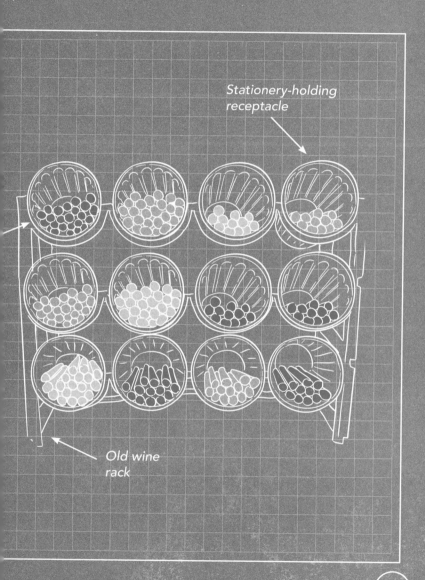

Stationery-holding receptacle

Old wine rack

BOOZY SHOES

Wine bottles can also be replaced by shoes. I have a cosmic collection of cool kicks and they all need to go somewhere. So I have devised a plan: have a party and drink up all the wine in a large rack, then put your very coolest sneakers inside the empty slots. Display the rack in your hallway or bedroom and impress your guests with your taste and style, not to mention it's an easier way for storing shoes.

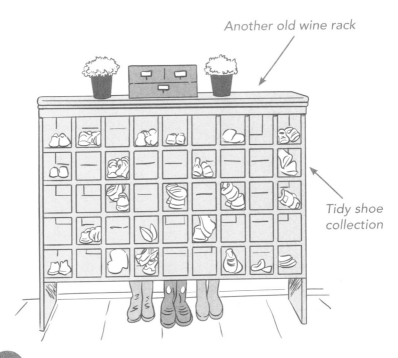

Another old wine rack

Tidy shoe collection

A KITCHEN-ESSENTIALS UNIT

As you may have already gathered, wine racks make great cubby holes for storing many things that are not actually wine. So instead of splashing the cash on storage units for each room, why not use the wine rack as a means of storage? You could put up a rack on the kitchen wall and use it for those odds and ends that could clutter the kitchen: tea towels, shopping notepads, oven gloves, bags–all can go in the wine rack. If you feel like treating yourself, perhaps you could afford to lose one slot to a sneaky bottle of vino. Just tell everyone you need it for the risotto!

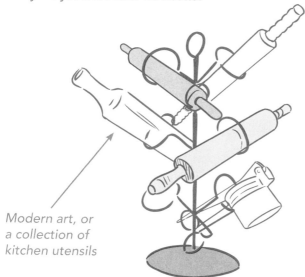

Modern art, or a collection of kitchen utensils

ARTS-AND-CRAFTS HACKS

If you are an arty type, then you will own all kinds of stuff that gets tangled easily, lost, broken, blunt… I'm not really selling the creative hobbies here, am I? I've got the answers for all your arts-and-crafts conundrums. Don't worry about losing the end of your tape, or where your ribbons have attached themselves to, for *Tidy Hacks* is here.

RIBBON HACK

Ribbon enthusiasts, this is a perfect hack for you. Like me, you will collect large amounts of ribbon. I am artistically talented and creating ribbon collages and wrapping presents professionally are just some of my favorite pastimes.

By using a plastic basket and two dowel rods you'll be able to store them, knot-free and on a reel. Simply slide on your ribbon wheels along the dowel rod, thread the ribbon through the gaps in the plastic basket, and then slot the dowel rod into the basket too. That way the ribbon can be easily pulled through when creating masterpieces and kept safe when not.

Holy plastic basket, Batman

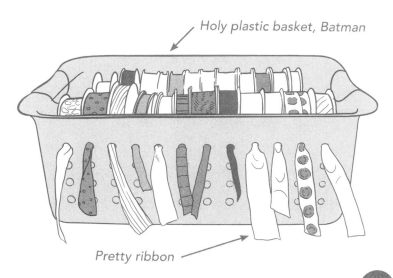

Pretty ribbon

EGG CARTON SEWING KIT

There has been an emergency. A repair needs to be made to my favorite fringe vest. I reach for the sewing stuff but the exact shade of thread is knotted up with the red, and the sewing needles are nowhere to be seen. The fringe vest had to be thrown away as it has now unraveled beyond repair. To stop this from ever happening again I came up with a nifty sewing box idea.

To keep your sewing equipment all in one place, you will just need an egg carton. Use some of the compartments to create little pillows for pins, needles, and buttons (using a scrap of fabric wrapped around some padding and glued in place). Use the rest to store thread, thimbles, and measuring tape. Close the lid shut and put the kit away until the next emergency.

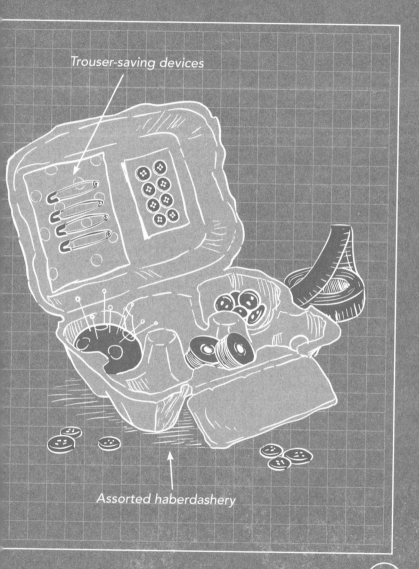

Trouser-saving devices

Assorted haberdashery

TAPE TAG

Do you spend hours trying to find the end of your duct tape? Frustrating, isn't it? Even when you do find it, you virtually rip off a fingernail trying to peel the darn stuff back. Preserve your manicure with this simple trick. You know those colored plastic tabs you get on bagged loaves of bread? Don't throw the tabs away. Attach one to the end of your duct tape or masking tape and you'll be able to locate the end in a nanosecond, leaving you more time to enjoy duct-taping the side-view mirror back on!

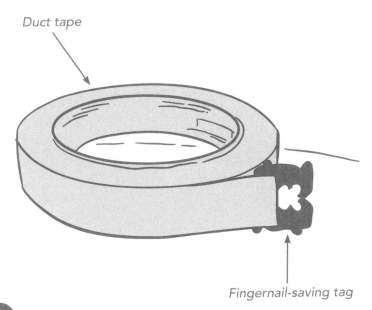

Duct tape

Fingernail-saving tag

CUTTING-EDGE TECHNOLOGY

The title makes this hack sound like it's high tech, but it really isn't. It's a quick and easy way to sharpen your blunt scissors.

Simply fold up a few layers of aluminium foil and cut through it several times. Each time a dull pair of scissors is cut through the foil the blades will sharpen. You can now trim your nose hair (and perform other related household cutting jobs) with ease!

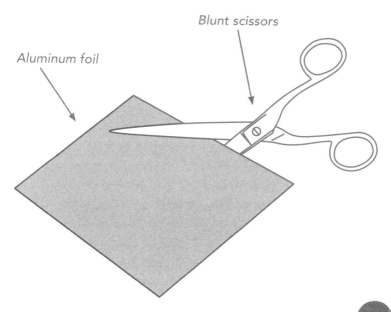

Blunt scissors

Aluminum foil

DIY
HACKS

Can't stand the thought of DIY? Well, *Tidy Hacks* is here to save the day. Unfortunately, you'll still have to do it, but with these ingenious ideas, drilling and hammering without breaking any serious health and safety rules has never been easier.

FLUFFY-SOCK PROTECTOR

Perhaps you own a vast collection of Ming vases or a huge number of glass miniatures, or maybe you've inherited a family of china cats that you can't stand the sight of but you want to keep for sentimental reasons, then you need this hack.

Simply place your precious china and glass figurines in individual fluffy socks and put them in a safe place or a box out of sight!

Ming dynasty heirloom

A warm sock

THUMB SAVER PART ONE

How to solve the age-old problem of hitting your thumb while hammering? Easy-peasy–in fact, so easy that there are two solutions.

To avoid blackening your thumbs, use a clothespin to hold the nail in place before you strike it. Then you can thrash away with your hammer until the nail is firmly in place.

CAUTION: This hack will not help you if your aim is so bad that it bends the nail, in which case use a screw or buy a nail gun. On second thought, if your aim is *that* bad, don't buy a nail gun....

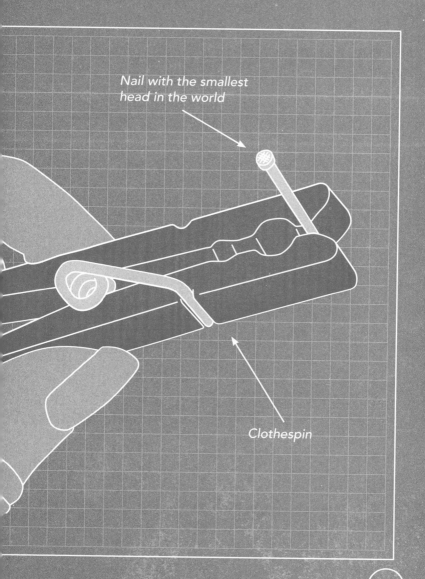

Nail with the smallest
head in the world

Clothespin

THUMB SAVER PART TWO

The second way of solving this problem is for those without access to a clothespin. (How do you people dry your clothes?!) Simply take a comb and hold the nail in place by wedging it between two of the teeth. Don't tell me you don't comb your hair either?

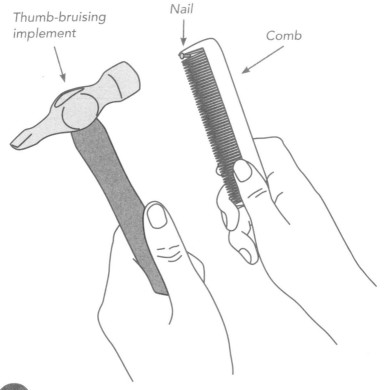

Thumb-bruising implement

Nail

Comb

WOOD CRAYON FILLER

It's frustrating when you bang a hole in the wrong bit of wall or woodwork. Usually when this happens you would visit the DIY shop and purchase a wax filler, but what you might not realize (forehead-slap moment) is that there are wax sticks in every color imaginable, right in your home. So I'm urging you, raid the children's bedroom/playroom for their wax crayons.

All you need to do is draw on the hole with the matching-color crayon until the nail hole is filled, rub away any excess with a soft cloth, and no one will ever suspect a thing.

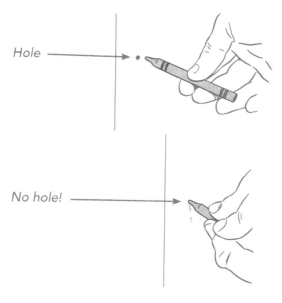

Hole

No hole!

NEAT GROUTING

The word *grouting* often evokes panic and deep distress; however, this little hack will have you grouting like a true tiler and with zero stress!

Stick painter's tape along each edge of where you need to put your sealant; this will act as your guide. You can be as messy as you want, the tape will protect the tiles underneath. Use your finger to shape and push out any excess, then peel away the tape to reveal some impressively neat lines.

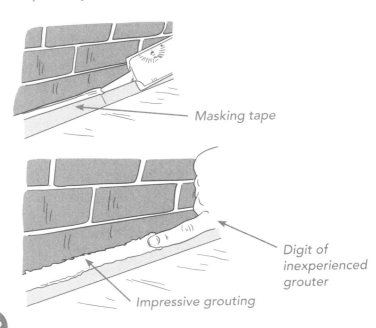

Masking tape

Digit of inexperienced grouter

Impressive grouting

PAINT BREAK

Repainting the walls is a necessary part in keeping the house looking spic-and-span. It can be thirsty work too, so what is there to do apart from take a break and have a warm cup of something? But while you are having a break, your paint is in danger of drying up and ruining your brush or roller. So don't forget to cover it with a plastic bag, tying it tightly to keep the paint damp inside. When you're ready to start painting again just remove the plastic bag and everything is ready to go! Simple!

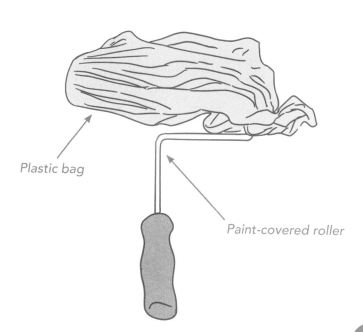

Plastic bag

Paint-covered roller

ANTI-DRIP PAINT CAN

Fans of painting and decorating will like this one. Wiping the excess paint off your brush onto the side of the can might seem like a good idea at the time but will result in paint buildup, which is messy and makes the lid stick when you try to replace it.

To solve this, place a rubber band across the opening of the can. This creates a handy scraper for wiping the excess paint off your brush. When you have finished painting, simply remove the elastic band and fit the lid back on with ease.

Paintbrush

Dirty rubber band, dripping with paint

Immaculate paint can

SCREWED SCREWS UNSCREWED

Who makes these screws with the heads that strip so easy? (No self-respecting dad should ever admit using too much force in this kind of situation—it was the screw, always the screw.) Well, anyway, there is a clever way to remedy the problem.

If your lame hardware has let you down yet again, grab yourself a rubber band and place it flat over the top of the screw head. Insert your screwdriver so it pins the band in place—now you have enough grip to get a proper purchase on the screw and finally get it out. Unless it breaks on you.

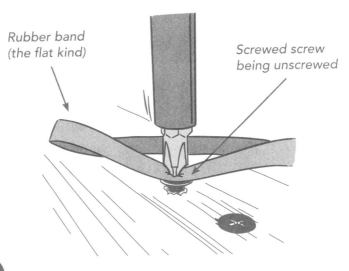

Rubber band
(the flat kind)

Screwed screw
being unscrewed

FINAL WORD

Congratulations, with my wisdom and your cooperation, you can now consider yourself a fully fledged tidying genius. You are now the master of every room in the house...and the garden too. Nothing can get in your way now. I would go as far as to say that you are kind of like a superhero. Okay, maybe that is a little much, but that's how I see myself.

So, with folding techniques in your mind and a wine rack as your right-hand man, the household will not know what's hit it—tidying, that's what.

Until next time, happy hacking!

INDEX

ACCESSORIES

DIY Bracelet Rack	**70-71**
Earring Grater	**63**
Hair Tie Organizer	**60**
Ice Cube Tray for Jewelry	**61**
Jewelry Fizz	**64-65**
Necklace Tangle Preventer	**67**
Sunglasses Rack	**69**
Teacup Jewelry	**62**

ARTS-AND-CRAFTS

Art-equipment Rack	**166-167**
Cutting-edge Technology	**175**
Egg Carton Sewing Kit	**172-173**
Ribbon Hack	**171**
Tape Tag	**174**

BATHROOM STORAGE

007 Towel Hanging	**46**
Fruit Basket Bathroom	**47**
Shower Storage	**44**
Space-saving Towel Storage	**45**
Tension Rod Hanger	**39**
Towel Hooks	**41**
Wino Towel Rack	**165**

BEDROOM

Duvet Burrito	**76-77**
Space-saving Scarf Hanger	**66**

CLEANING

Bathroom

Cleansing Bathroom Bombs	**54-55**
DIY Air Freshener	**53**
Grout De-grimer	**52**
Homemade Cleaner	**42-43**
Magic Lemons	**48-49**
Toothpaste Clip	**50**
Vinegar Toilet Cleaner	**51**

Bedroom

Ice, Ice Bedroom	**75**
Magic Water-ring Remover	**82-83**
Small-item Retrieval	**57**
Soda Water Stain Remover	**79**
Spray Away	**78**
Squeegee Dog-hair Remover	**81**
Teabag Wood Buffer	**80**
Vodka Mattress Disinfectant	**74**

Kitchen

Banish Kitchen Odors	**37**
Burnt-pan Cleaner	**34-35**

Cleaner Coffee	**32**
Drain Declogger	**31**
Grapefruit Oven Cleaner	**27**
Knife and Fork Rust Remover	**36**
Squeaky-clean Sponges	**33**
The Lazy Microwave-cleaning Trick	**26**
Tomato Polish	**28-29**
Quick-as-a-Flash Blender Cleaner	**38**

CLOTHING

Cardboard Cutouts	**105**
No-slip Hangers	**95**
Vertical Clothing	**73**
Wardrobe-expansion Kit	**72**

COMPUTER

Coffee Filter Screen Wipe	**89**

DIY

Fluffy-Sock Protector	**177**
Neat Grouting	**182**
Screwed Screws Unscrewed	**186**
Thumb Saver Part One	**178-179**
Thumb Saver Part Two	**180**
Wood Crayon Filler	**181**

DECORATING

Anti-drip Paint Can	**184-185**
Paint Break	**183**

ELECTRONICS

Binder Clip Cables	**108**
Cable Cases	**107**
Phone Charge Caddy	**110-111**
Smartphone Video-chat Stand	**92**
Stick-'em-up Remotes	**121**
Velcro Plugs	**24**

GARDENING
Equipment

Bungee Holdall	**133**
Garden-tool Rust Remover	**143**
Hose Stand	**127**
Milk Bottle Caddy	**130**
Sand Storage for Tools	**144**
Shed Magnets	**164**
Tool Caddy	**145**
Twine Dispenser	**128-129**

Flowers

Balloon Travel Vase	**149**
Marble Vases	**148**

Planting

Banana Fertilizer	**146-147**
Coffee Compost	**142**
Pithy Planters	**140-141**
Seedy Tape	**134-135**
Toilet-paper-roll Planters	**139**
Two-for-one Herbs	**138**

Storage
Chicken Feeder Shelf — 131
Garden Pegboard — 132
Seed Albums — 137
Seed Jars — 136

Weeds
Baking Soda Weed Killer — 126

GROOMING
Hair Grip Strip — 159
Makeup Brush Holder — 68
Makeup Magnets — 162

GENERAL STORAGE
Above-the-door Storage — 109
Bungee Shelf — 119
Cupcake Pan Organizer — 113
Egg Carton Storage — 112
Shoe Box Storage — 114
Shutter Space — 115
Twinkling Lights Up — 120

KIDS
Crayon Remover — 153
Dishwasher Art Rack — 154-155
Ice Pop-drip Catchers — 152
Mess-free Painting — 151
Glue Sponge — 157
Velcro Toy Storage — 156

KITCHEN STORAGE
Cupboards
Basket Space — 15
Garbage Bag Rollers — 21
Saucepan Lid Organizer — 30
Super Storage Hanger — 13

Fridge
Bookends for Beer Bottles — 16-17
Desk-to-Fridge Organizer — 141

General
A Kitchen-essentials Unit — 169
Magnets for Knives — 160-161

Jars
Cookie Jar — 18
Cupcake Liners Jam Jars — 20
Jammy Storage — 10-11
Spice Magnet — 163

Lunch-box
Pin-up Freezer Bag Boxes — 12

Surfaces
DIY Mail Board — 90-91
Over-the-Sink Chopping Board — 22-23

LAUNDRY
Bedding Hack — 94
Disappearing Deodorant Stains — 98
DIY Dryer Sheets — 100-101

Grass-stain Remedy   **104**
Grease-stain Remover   **99**
No-brainer Ironing Board Keeper **102**
No-crease Noodle   **96-97**
Odd Socks   **103**

MUSIC
Earphone Hack   **116-117**

PAPER
Wrap-up Hack   **118**

SECURITY
Color-coded Keys   **122-123**

SHOES
Boozy Shoes   **168**
DIY Shoe Hangers   **58-59**
Leather Scuff Eraser   **124**
Smelly Shoe Freshener   **84**

SHOPPING
Plastic Bag Dispenser   **25**

STATIONERY
Cereal Box Divider   **88**
Desk Hack   **87**
Jam Jar Pen Holders   **86**

WASTE MANAGEMENT
Easy-empty Garbage Can   **9**

WEALTH MANAGEMENT
Money Box   **19**